Chapter 1
Joseph Shivery

Chapter 2
Nancy Sutton Lewin

Chapter 3
Mr End

Chapter 4
Diane Pick-Ross

Chapter 5
Judy West

Chapter 6
Arthur Santiago

Chapter 7
Shelly Eartha Simpson

Chapter 8
Dawn Miller

Chapter 9
Alexandra Rodriguez

Chapter 10
Laurie Beauchamp

Chapter 1
Joseph Shivery

USA
Facebook : The-Broken-Mind-of-Joes-Ink

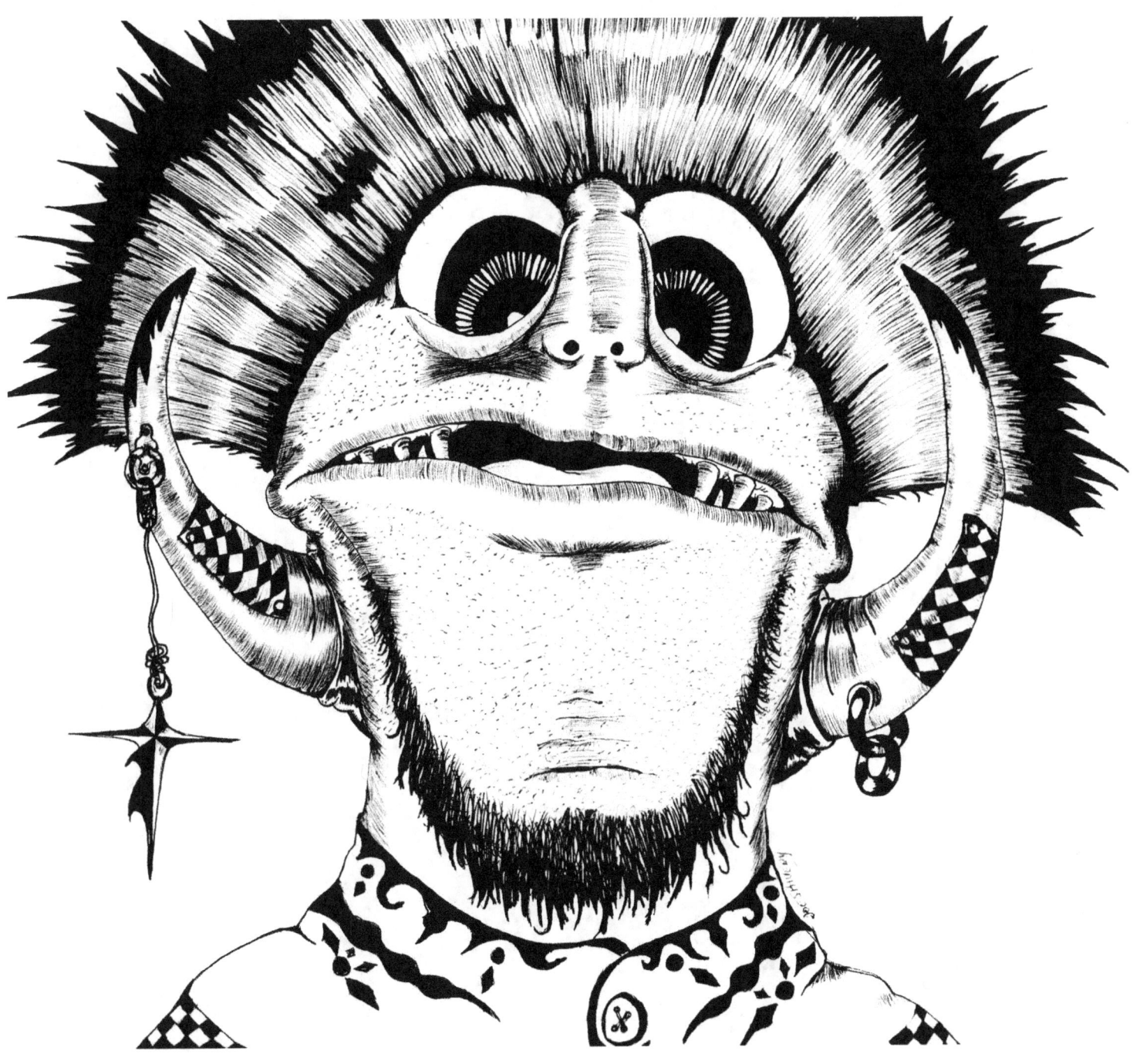

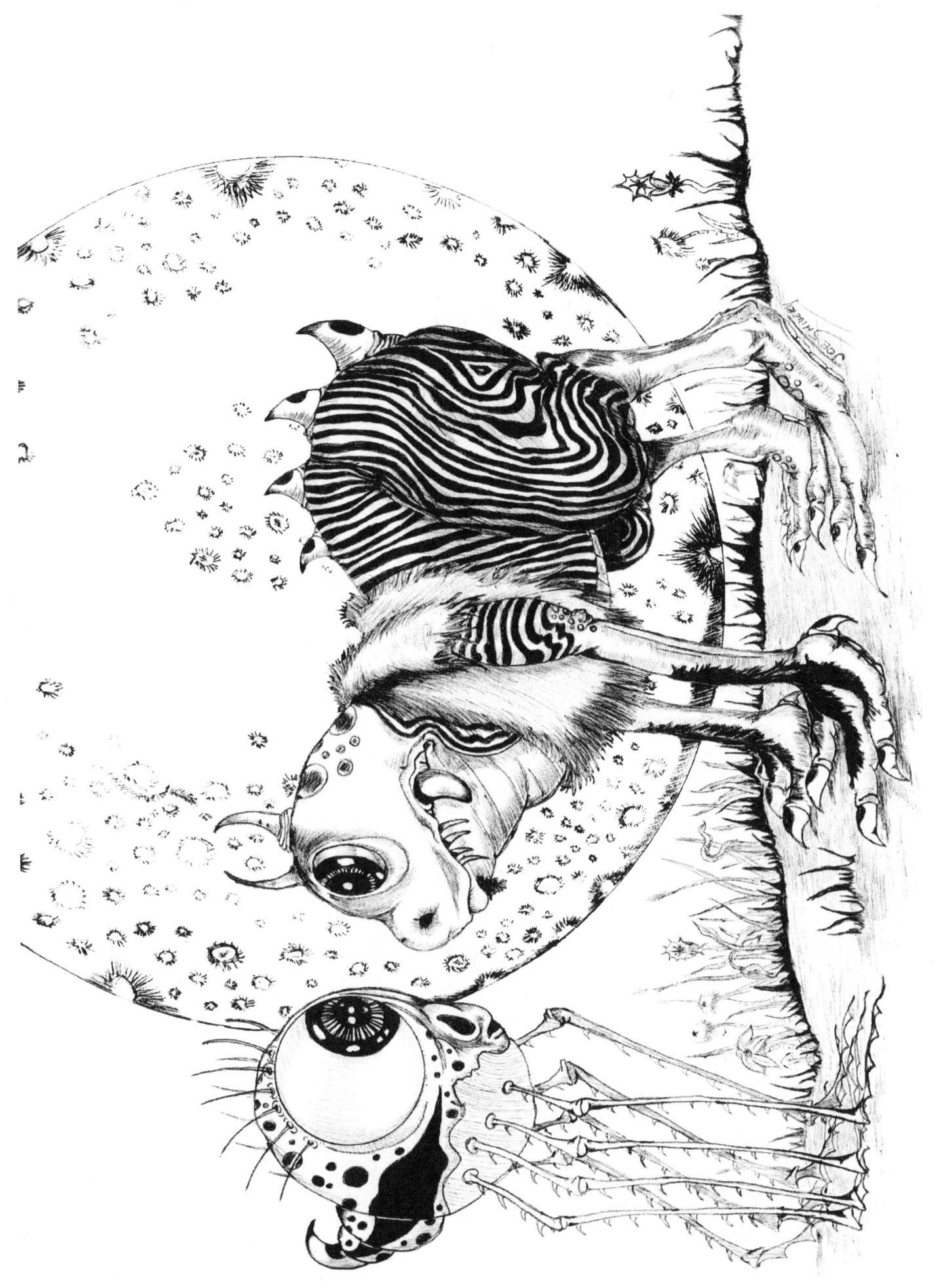

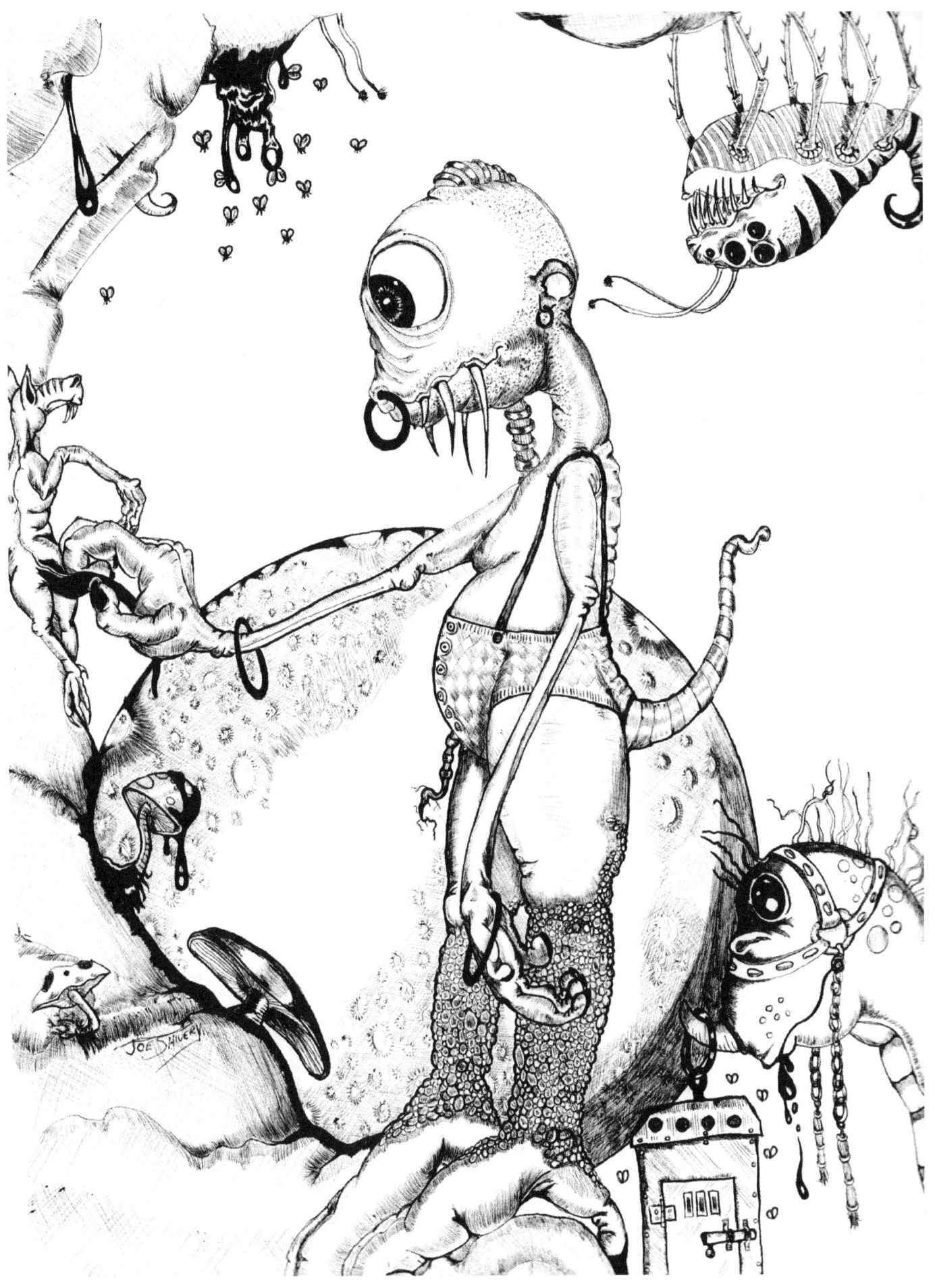

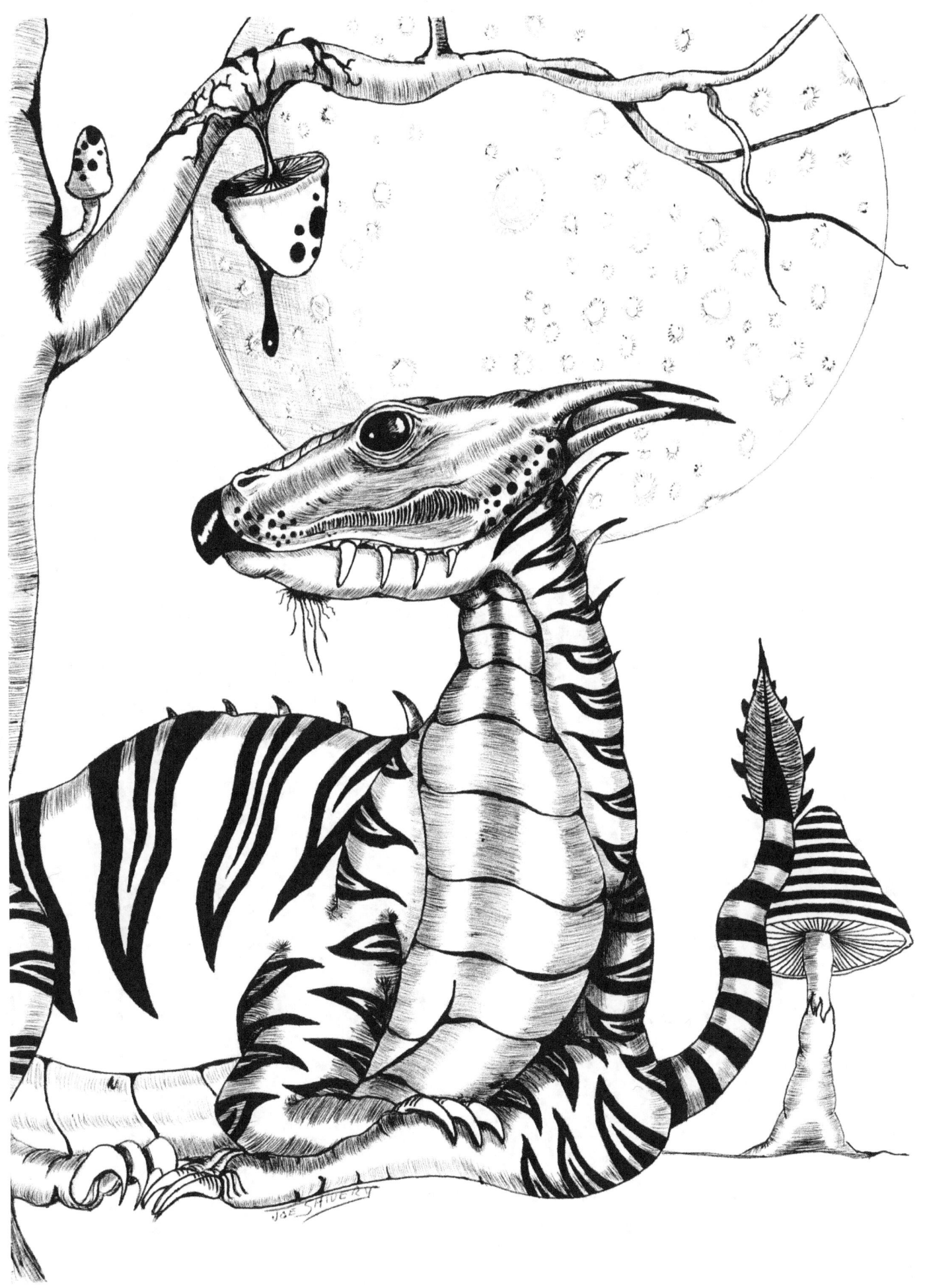

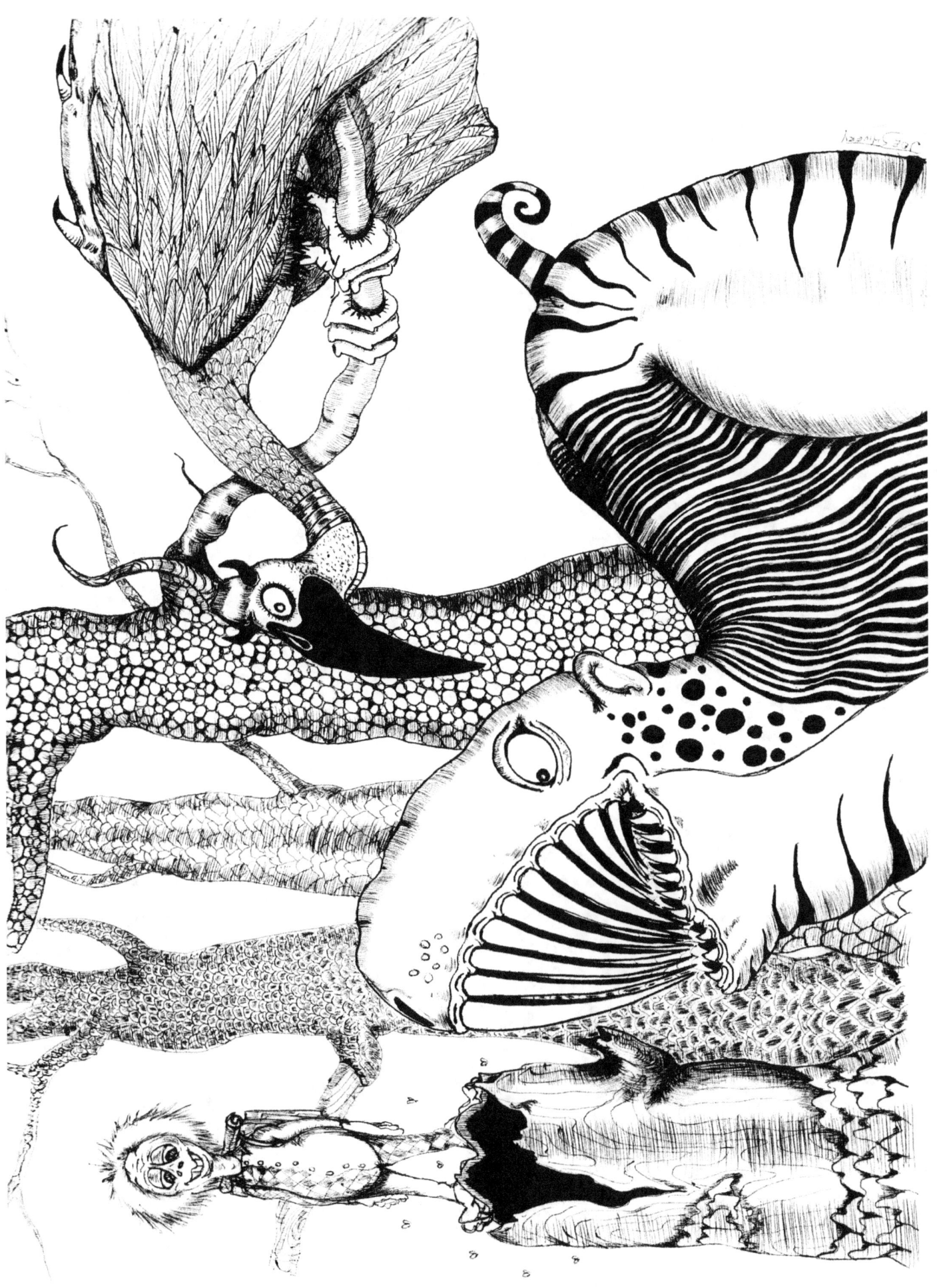

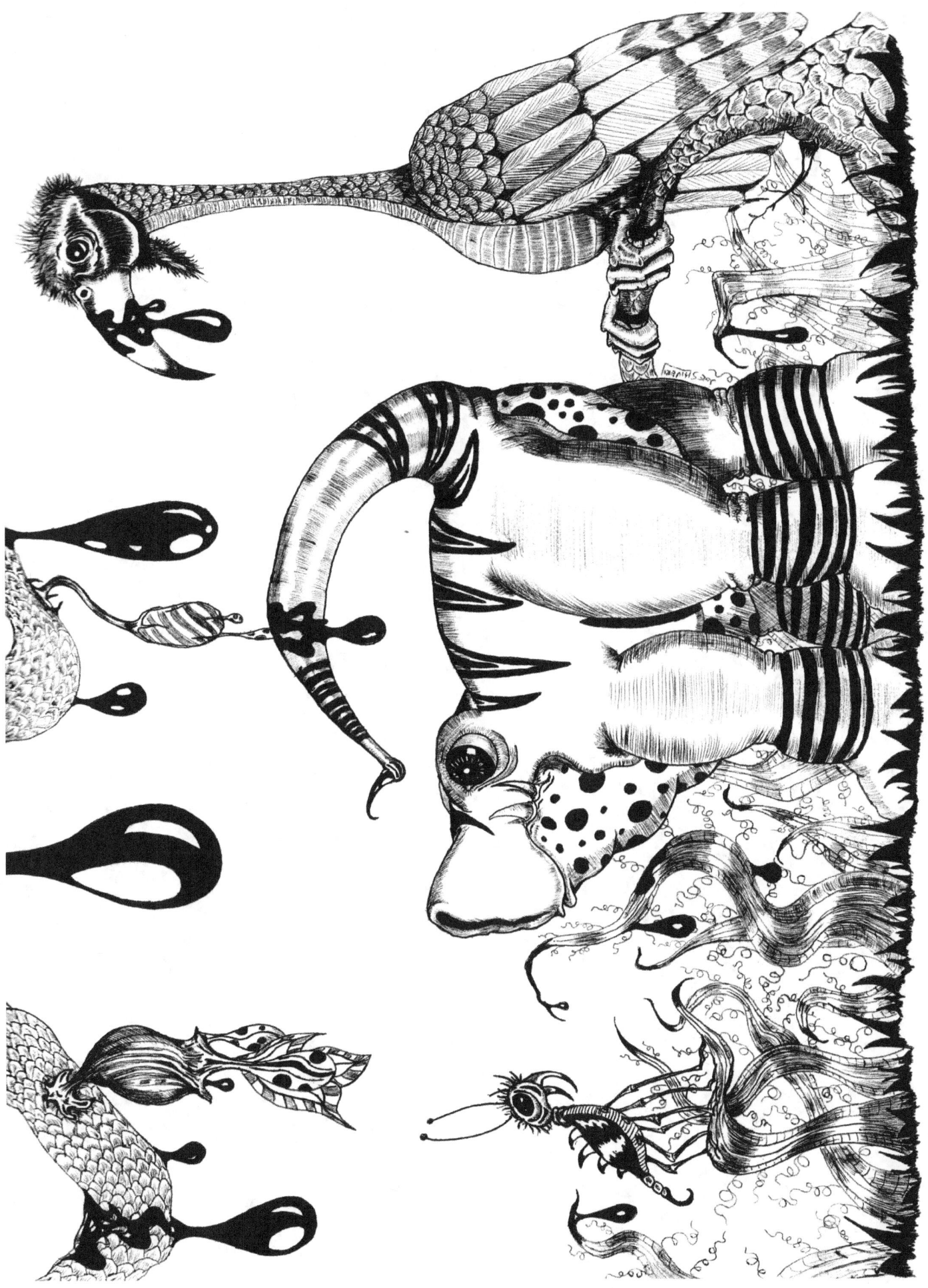

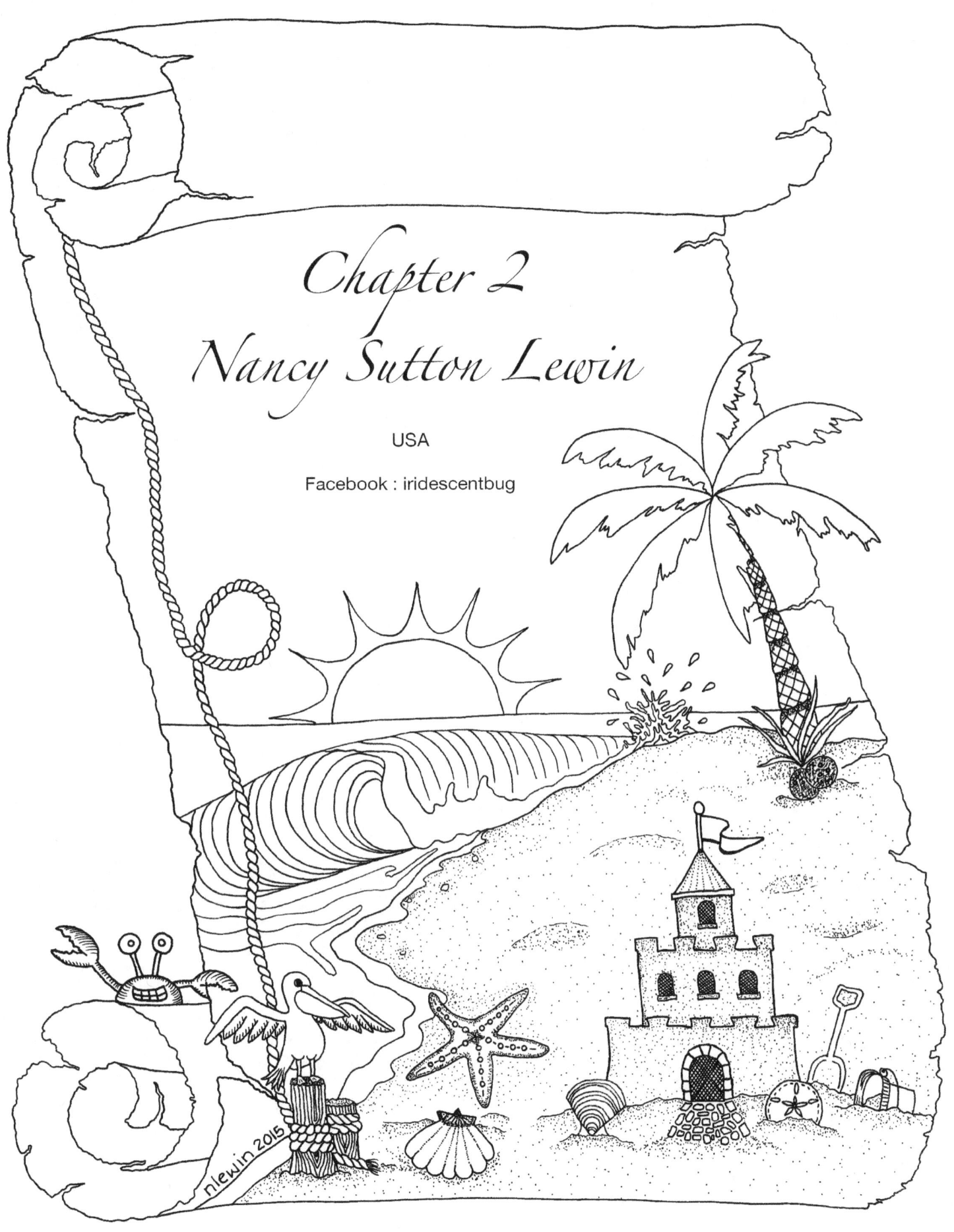

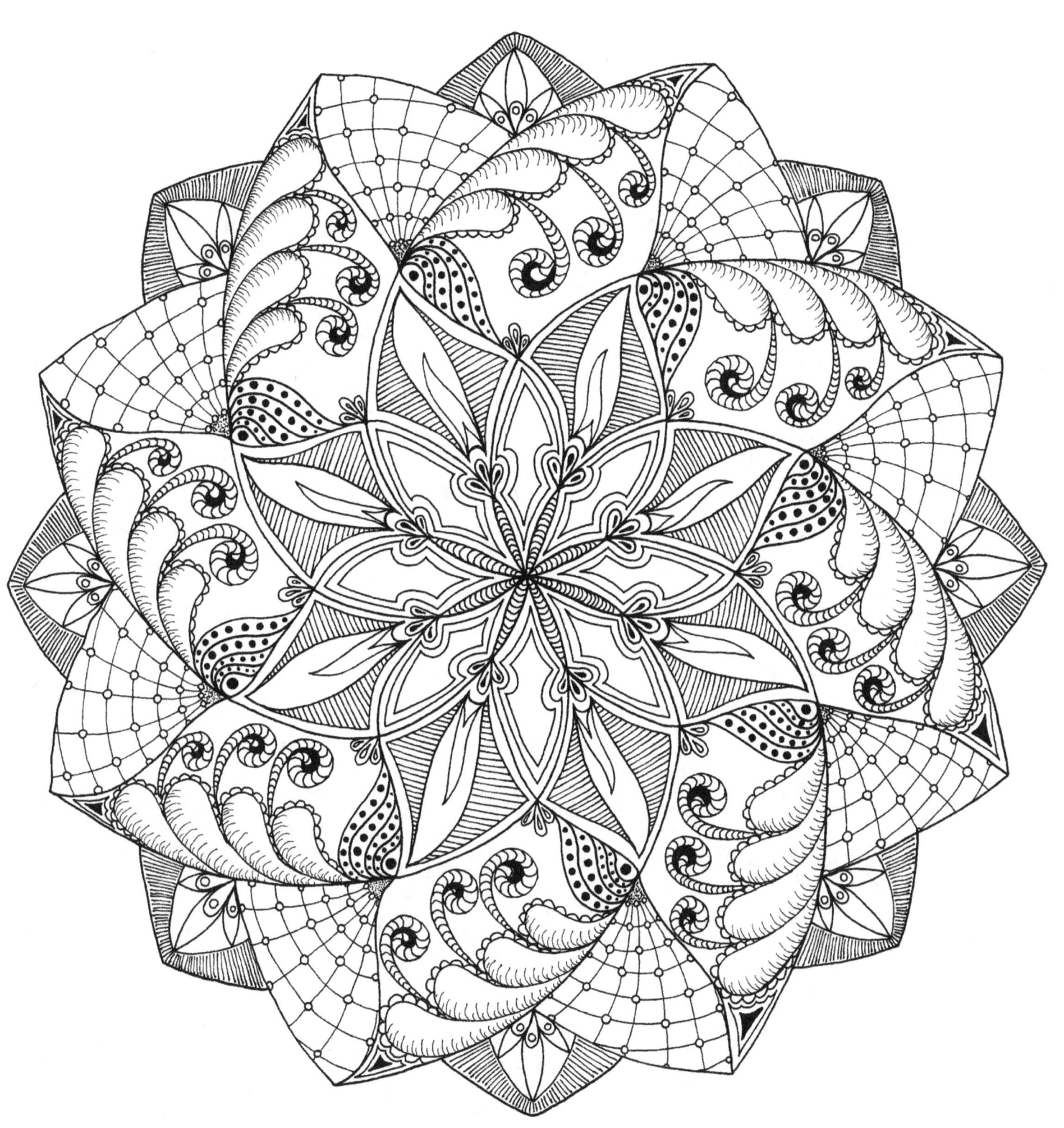

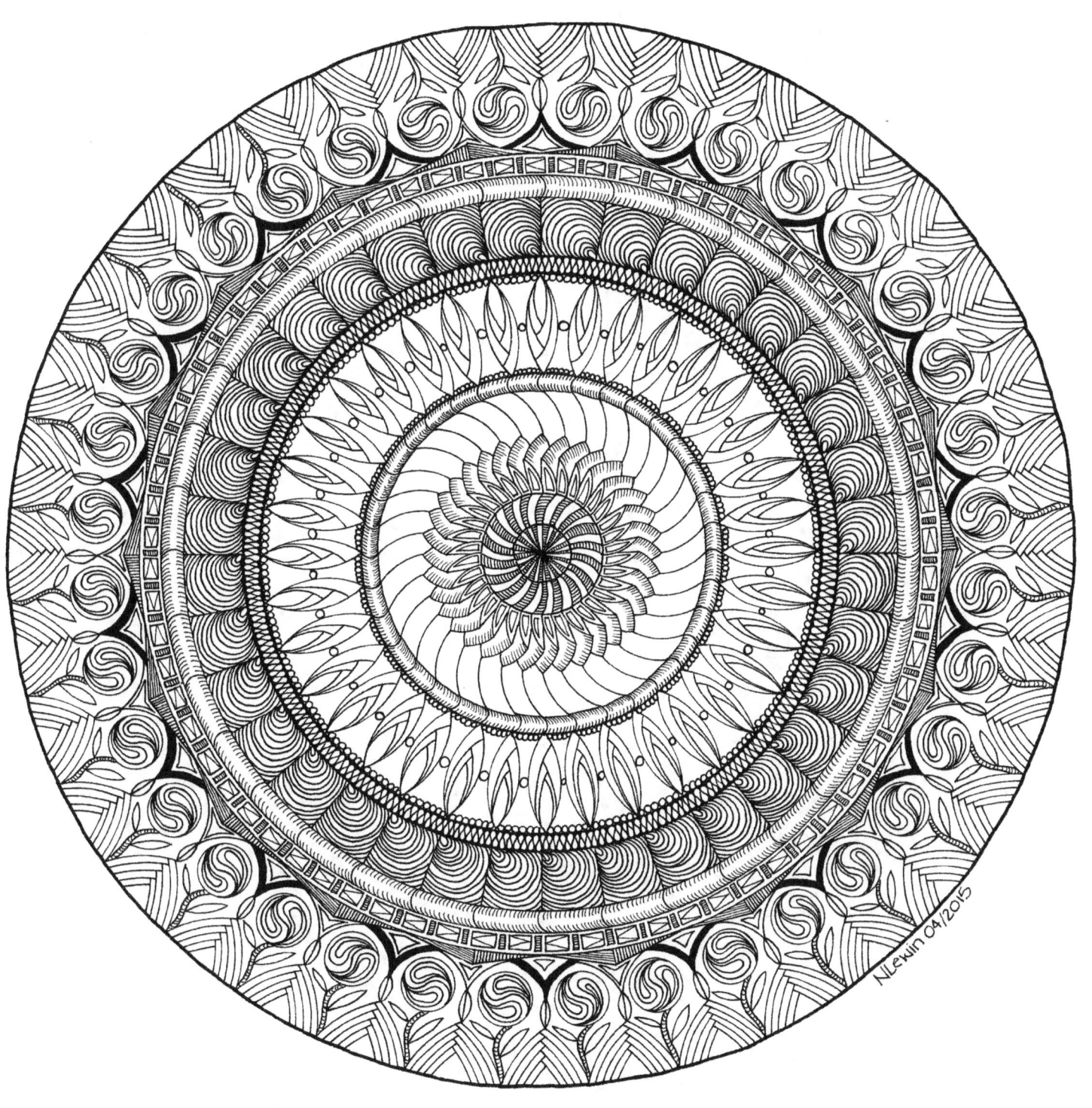

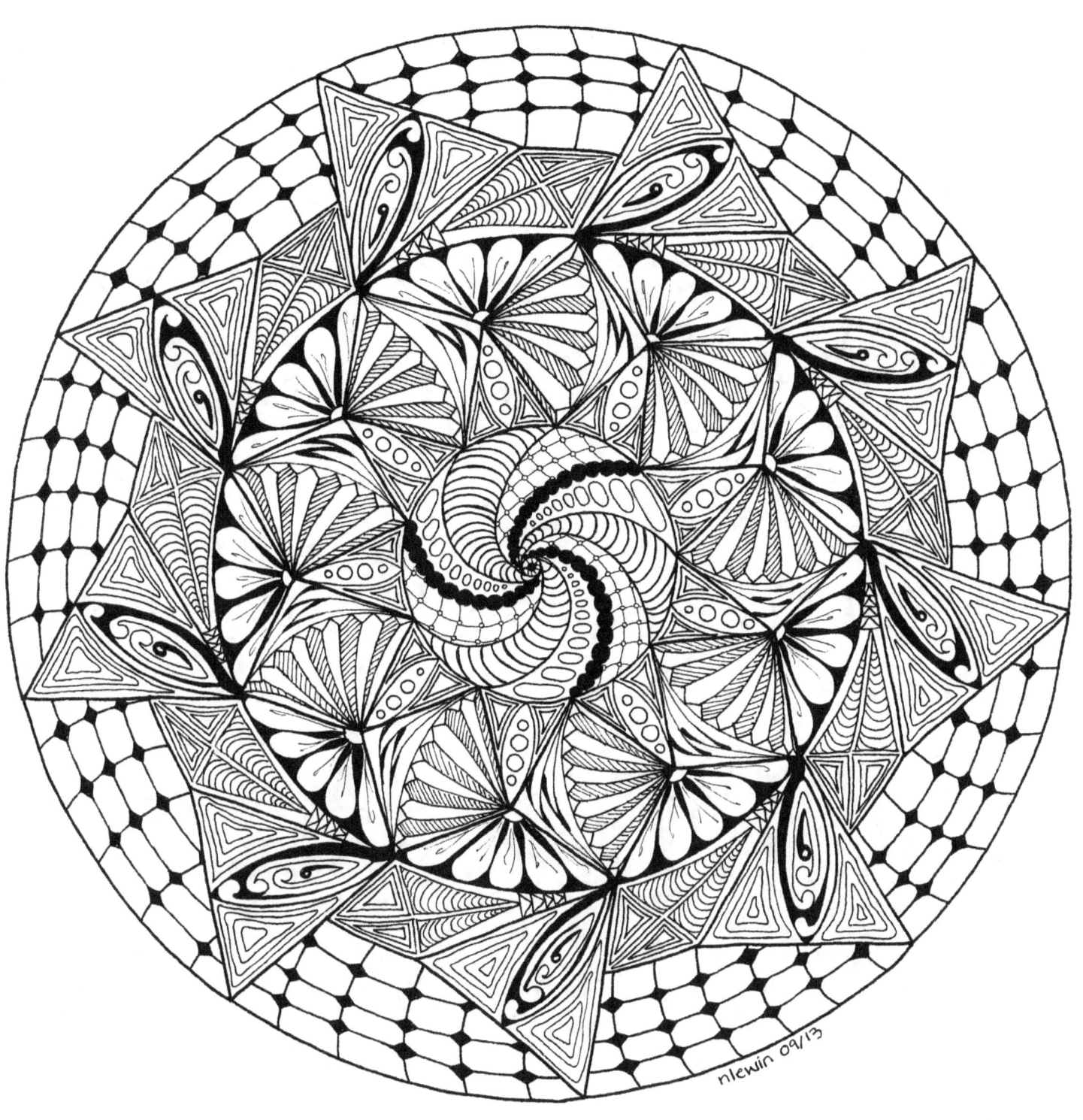

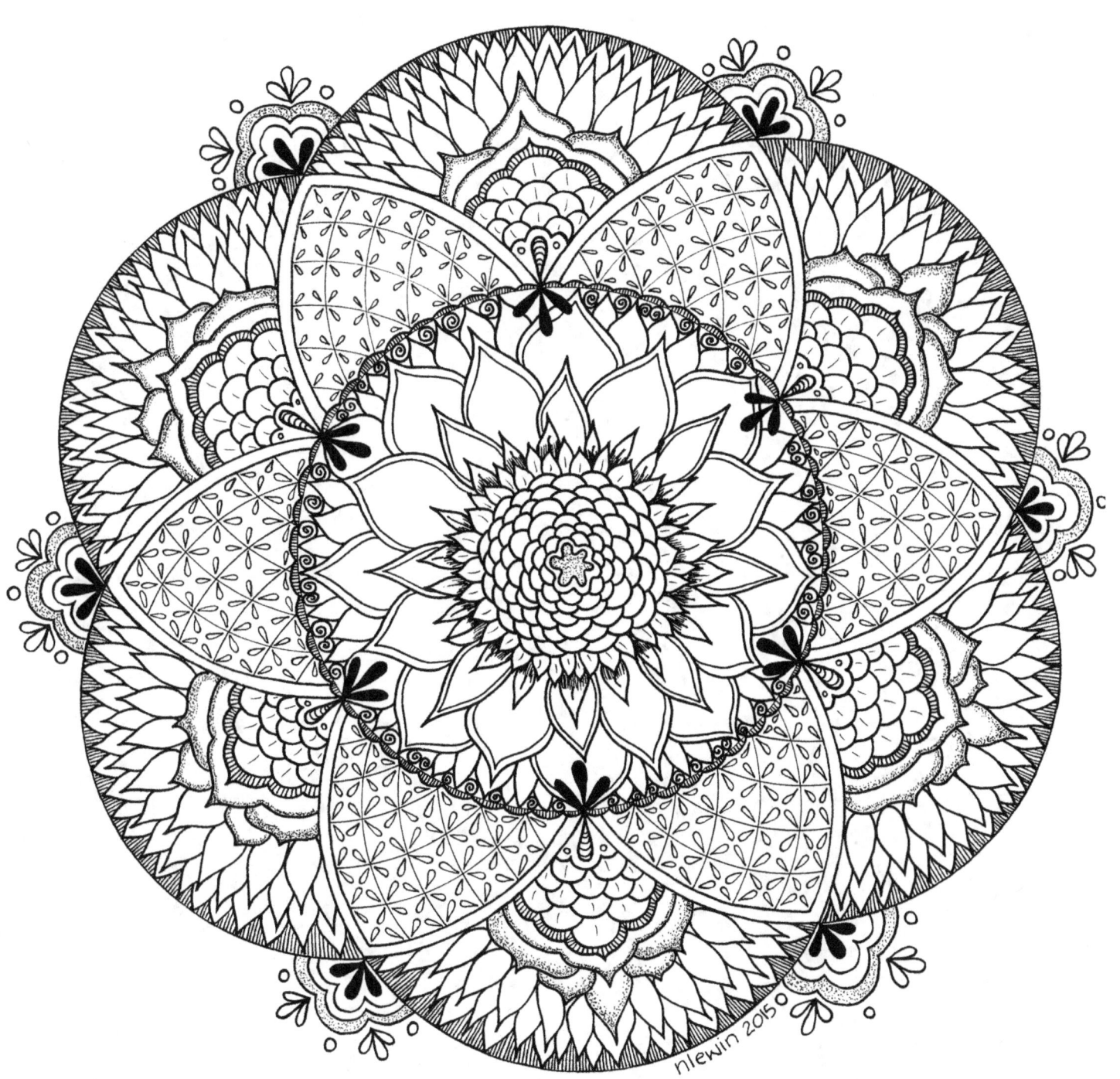

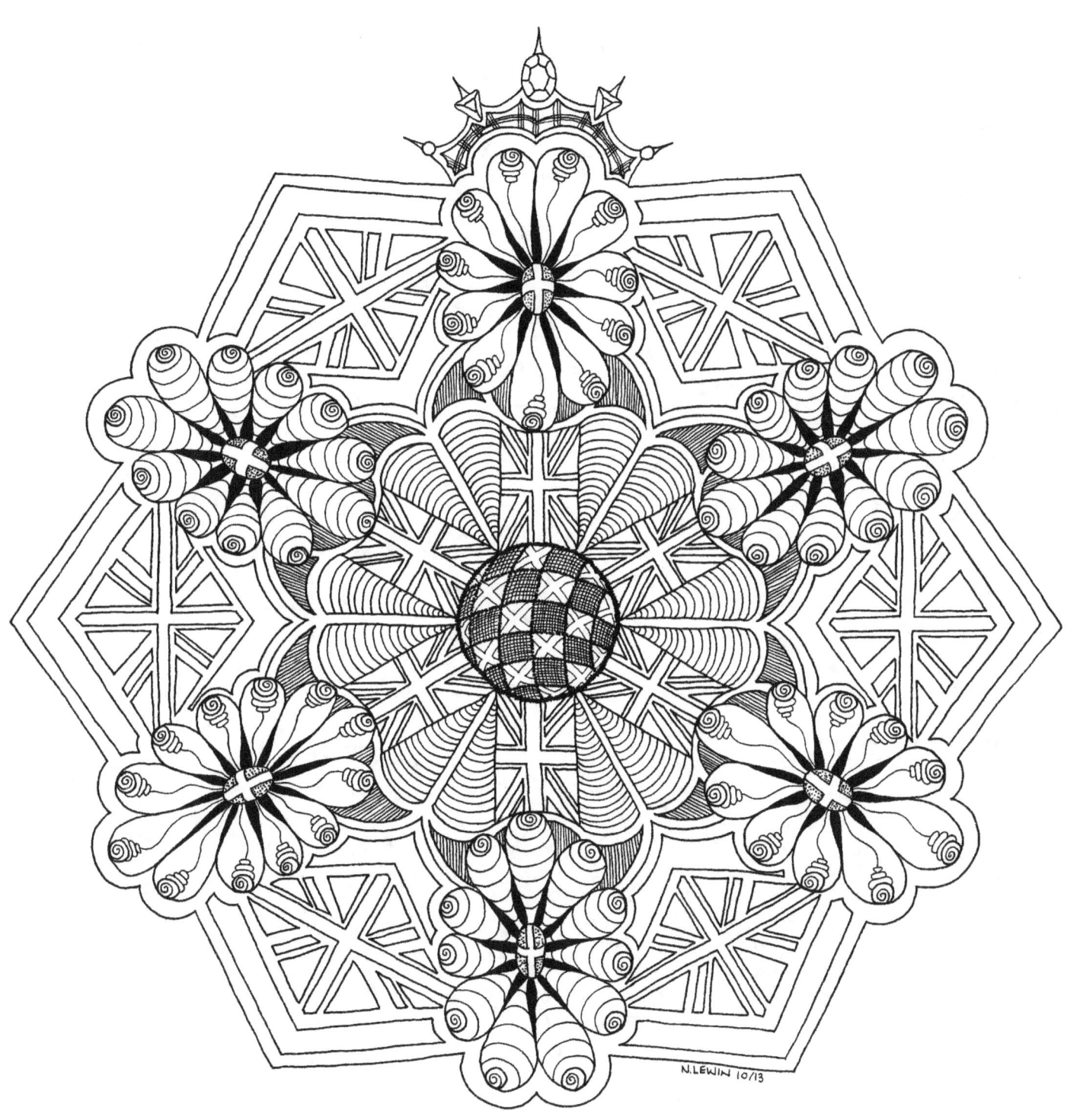

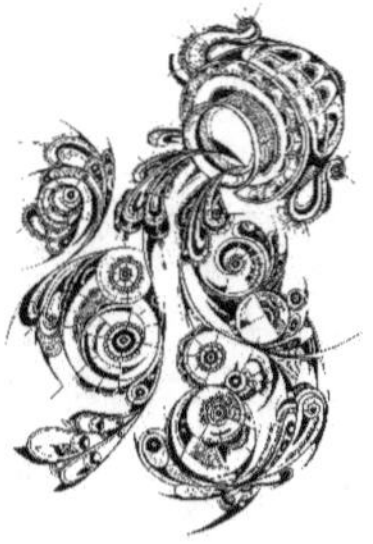

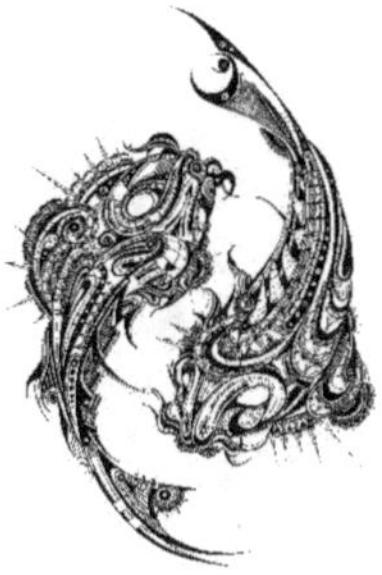

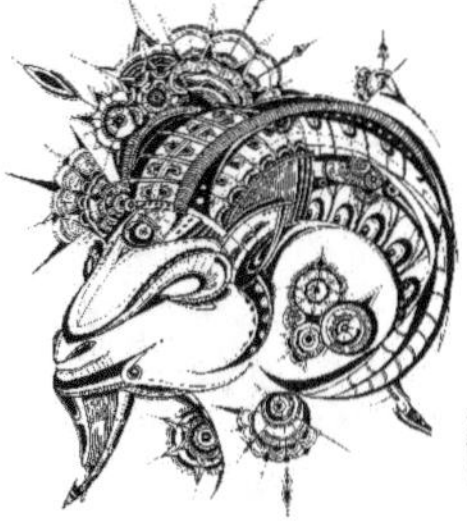

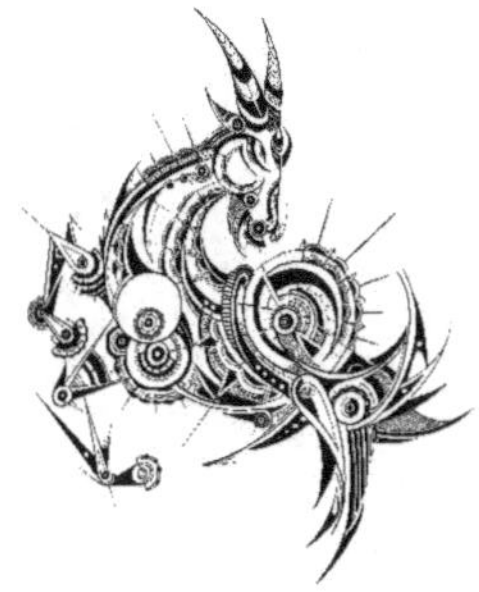

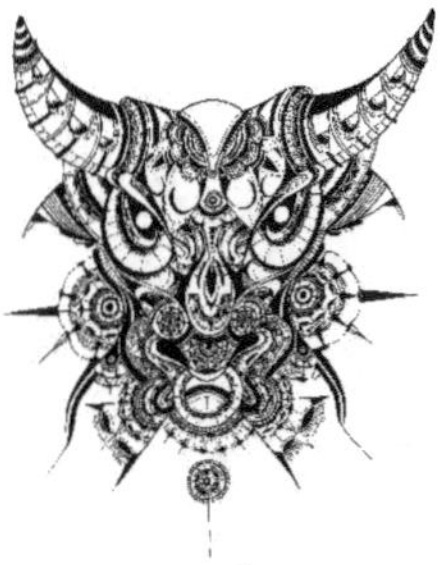

Chapter 3
Mr.End Horoscope

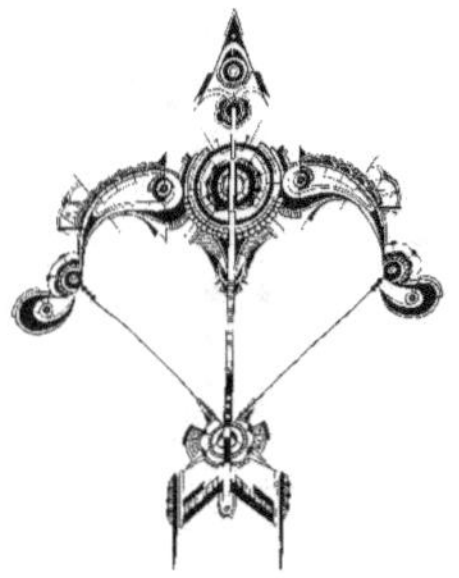

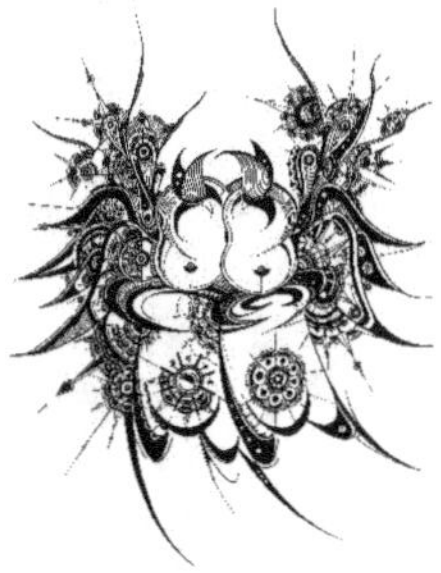

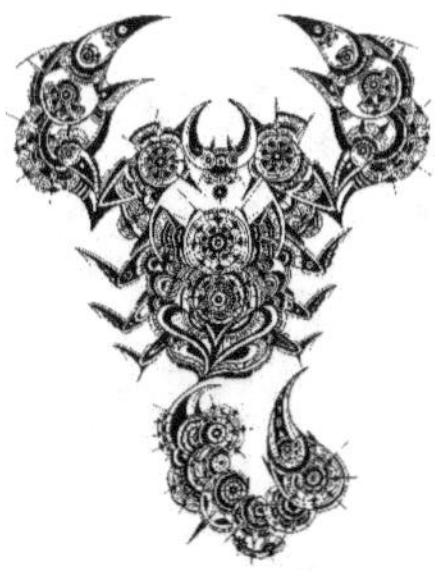

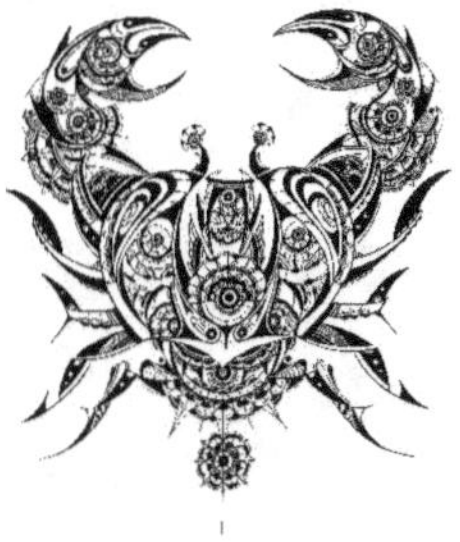

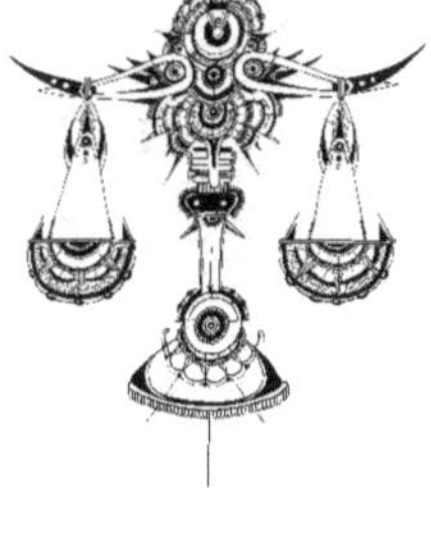

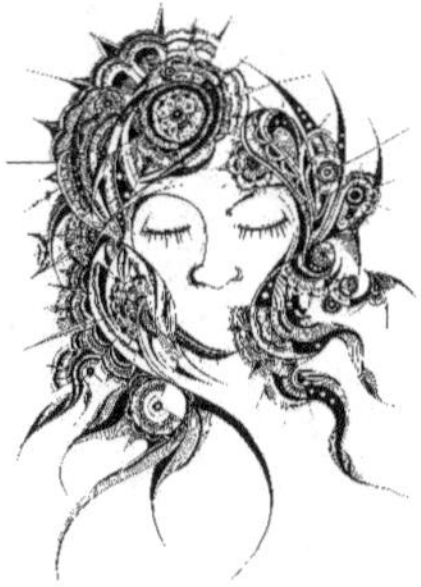

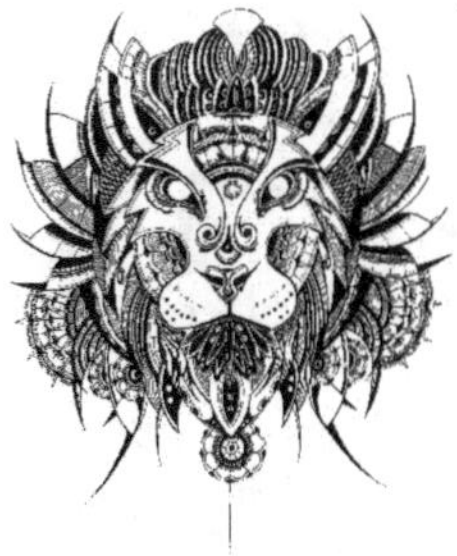

www.facebook.com/
GeometryFlow

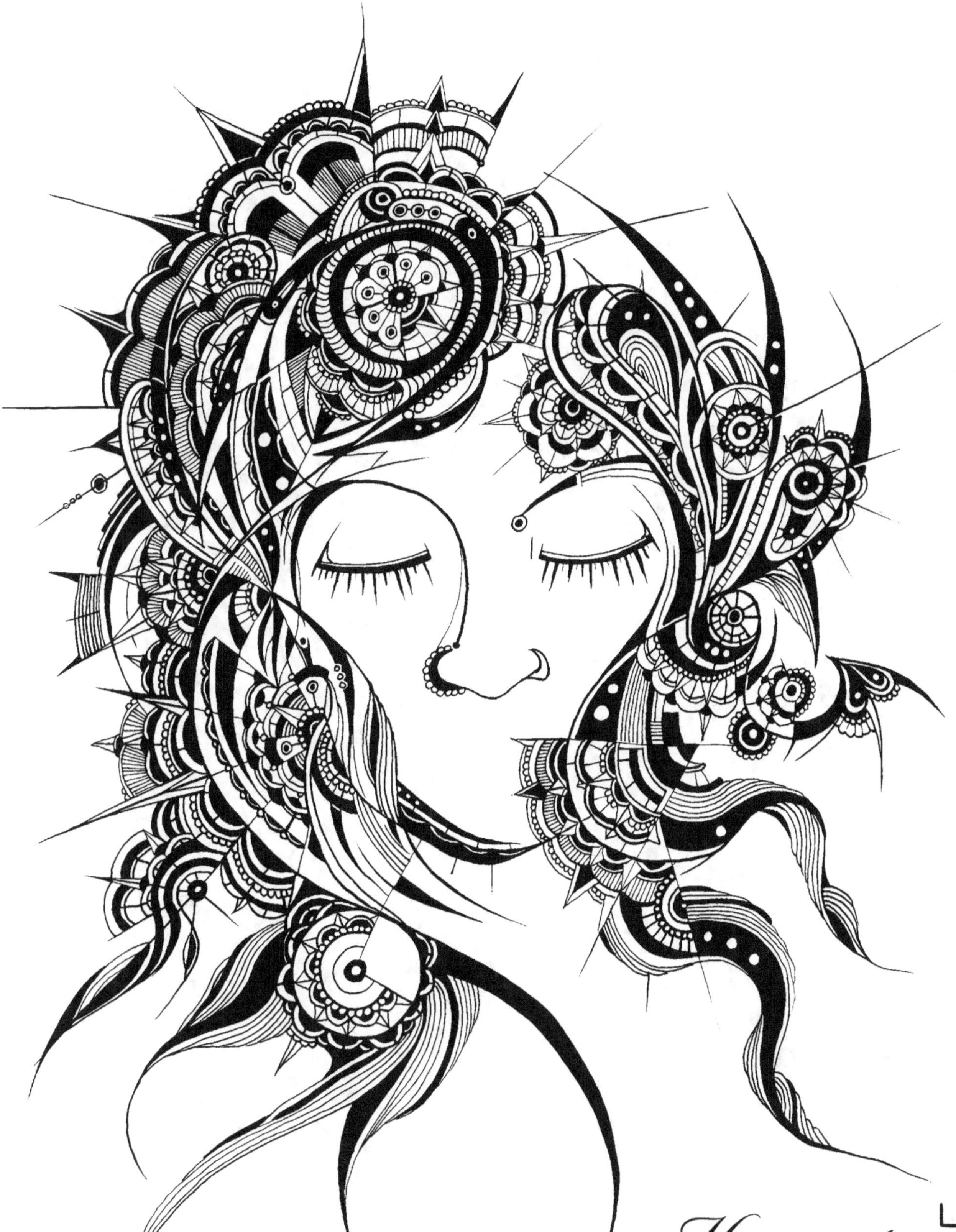

Horoscope
VIRGO
Mr.End

www.facebook.com/
GeometryFlow

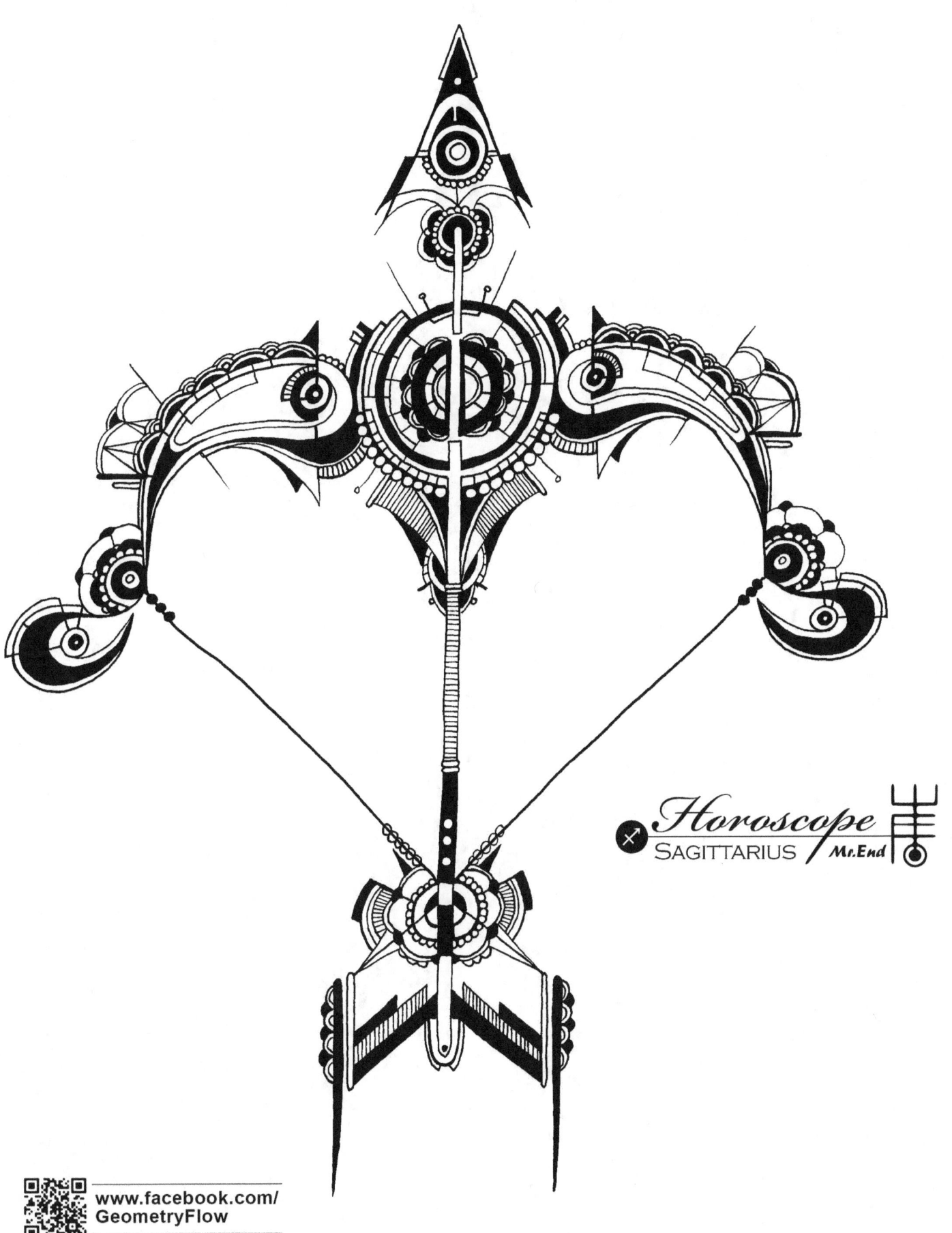

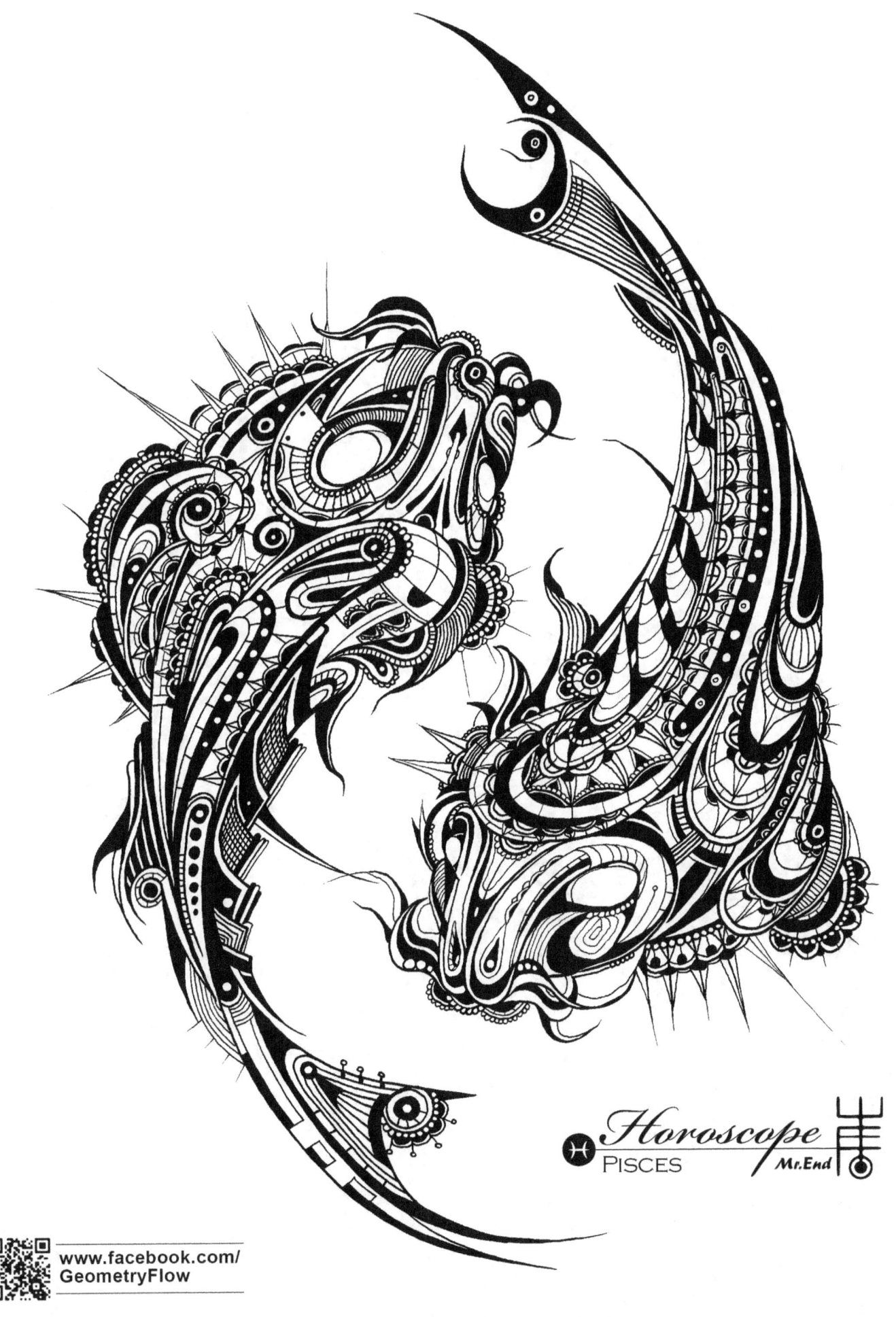

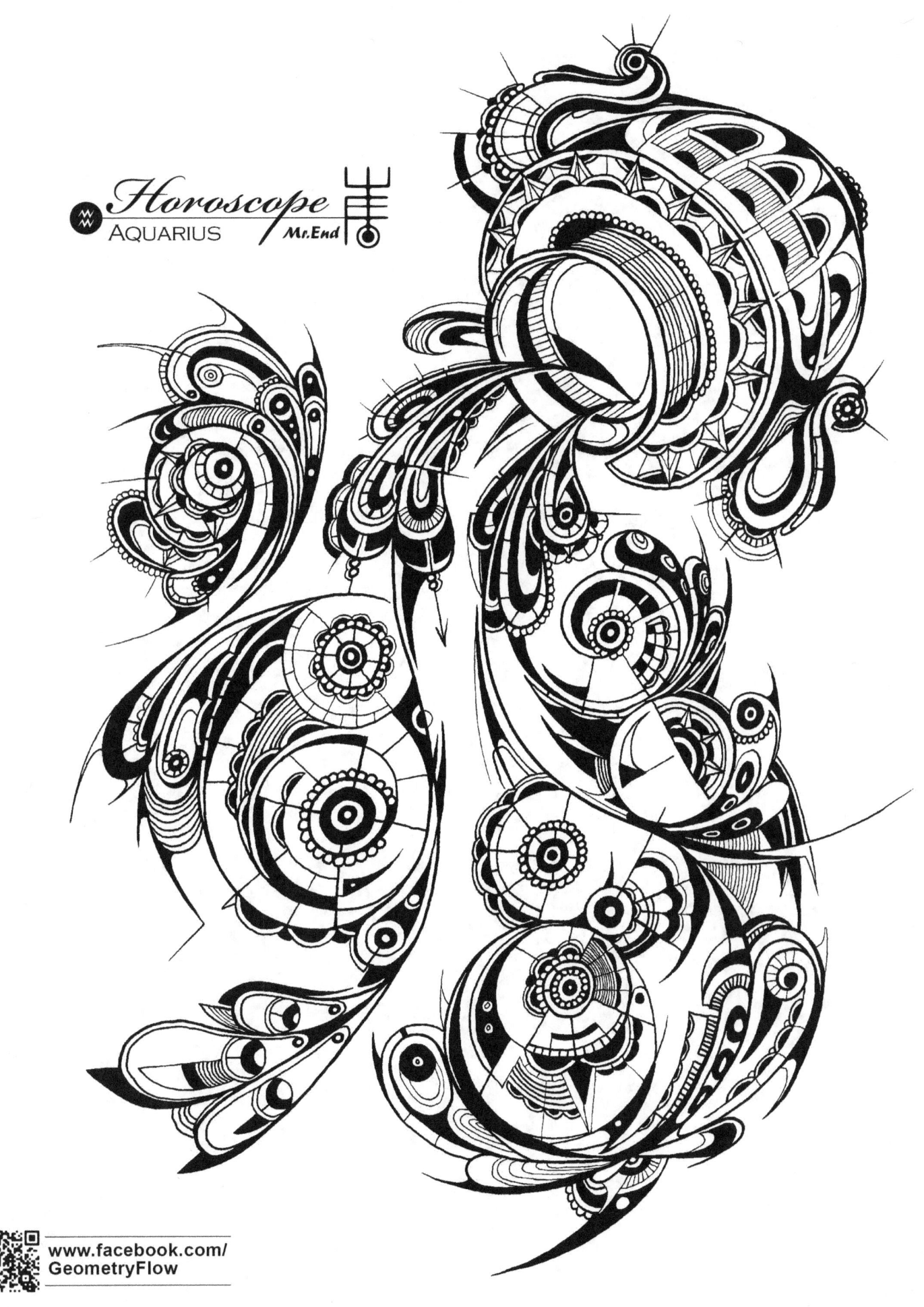

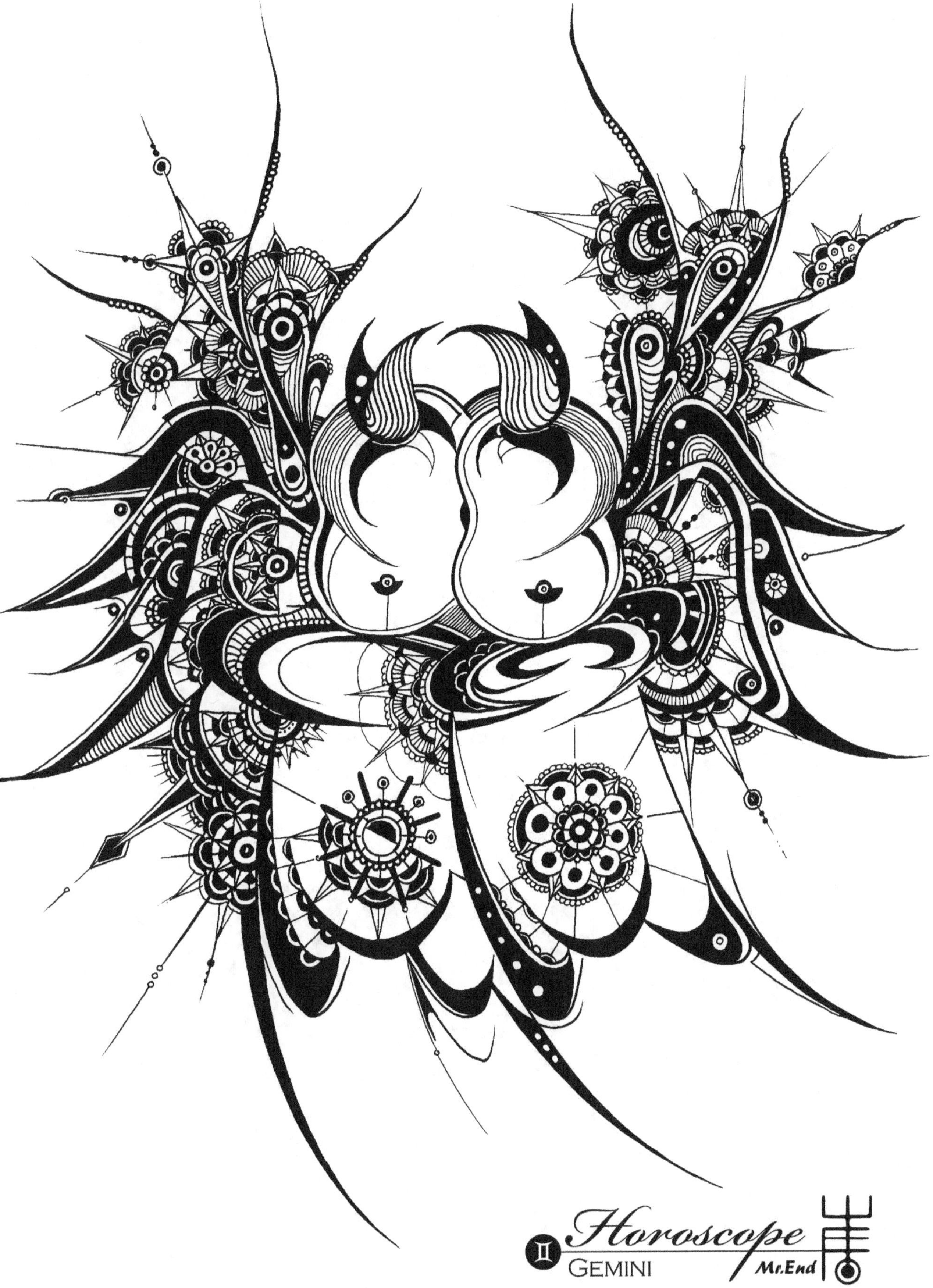

www.facebook.com/
GeometryFlow

Horoscope
GEMINI — Mr.End

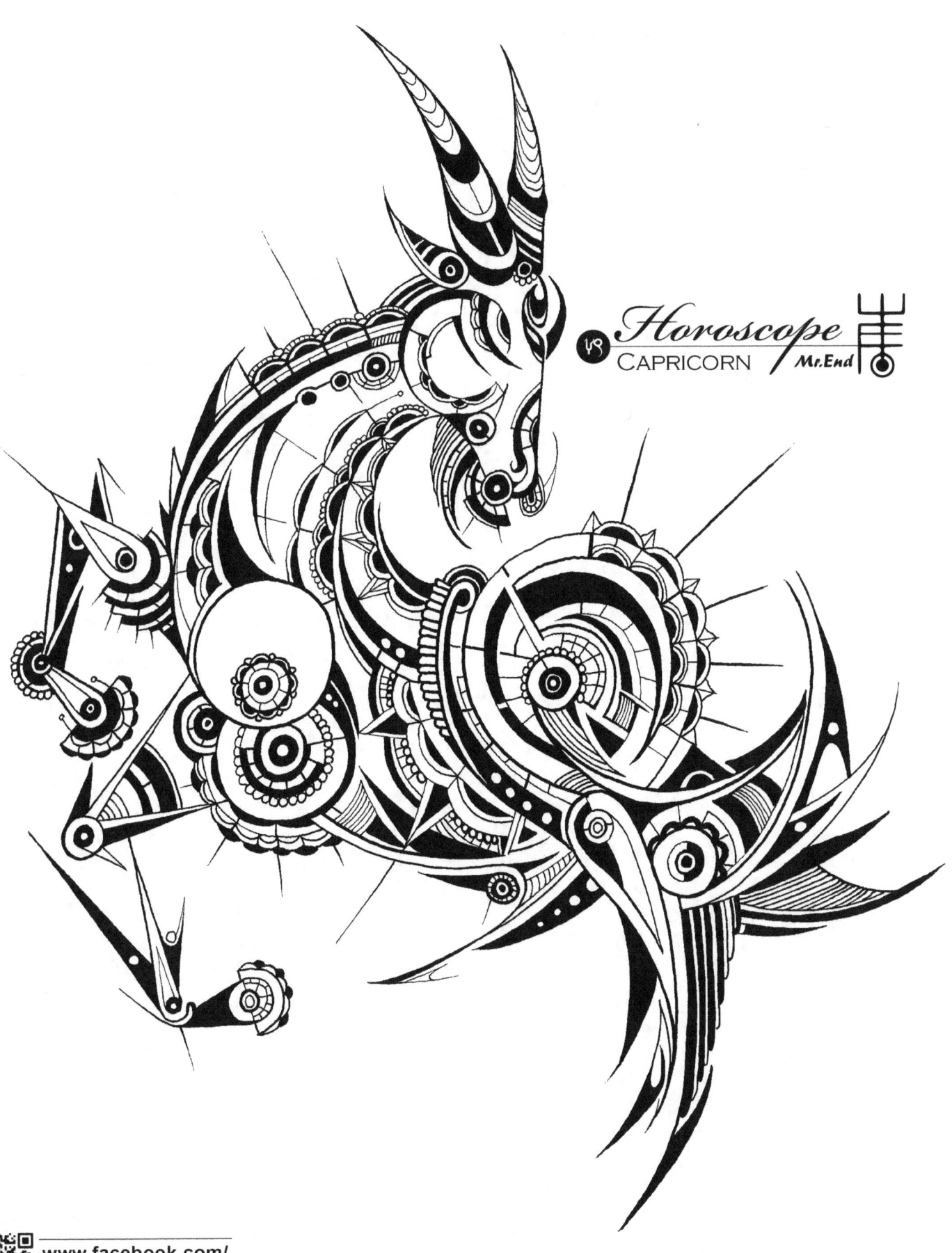

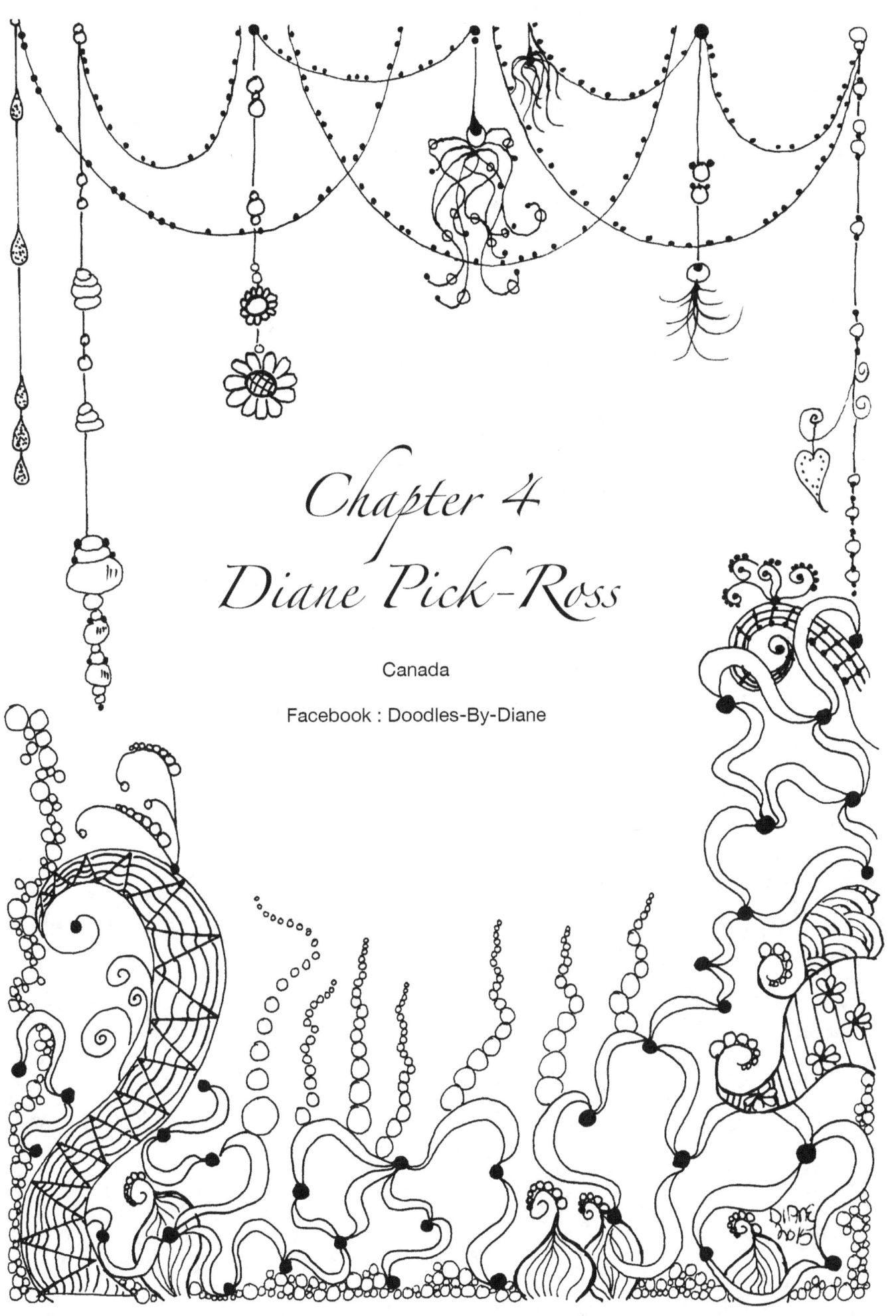

Chapter 4
Diane Pick-Ross

Canada

Facebook : Doodles-By-Diane

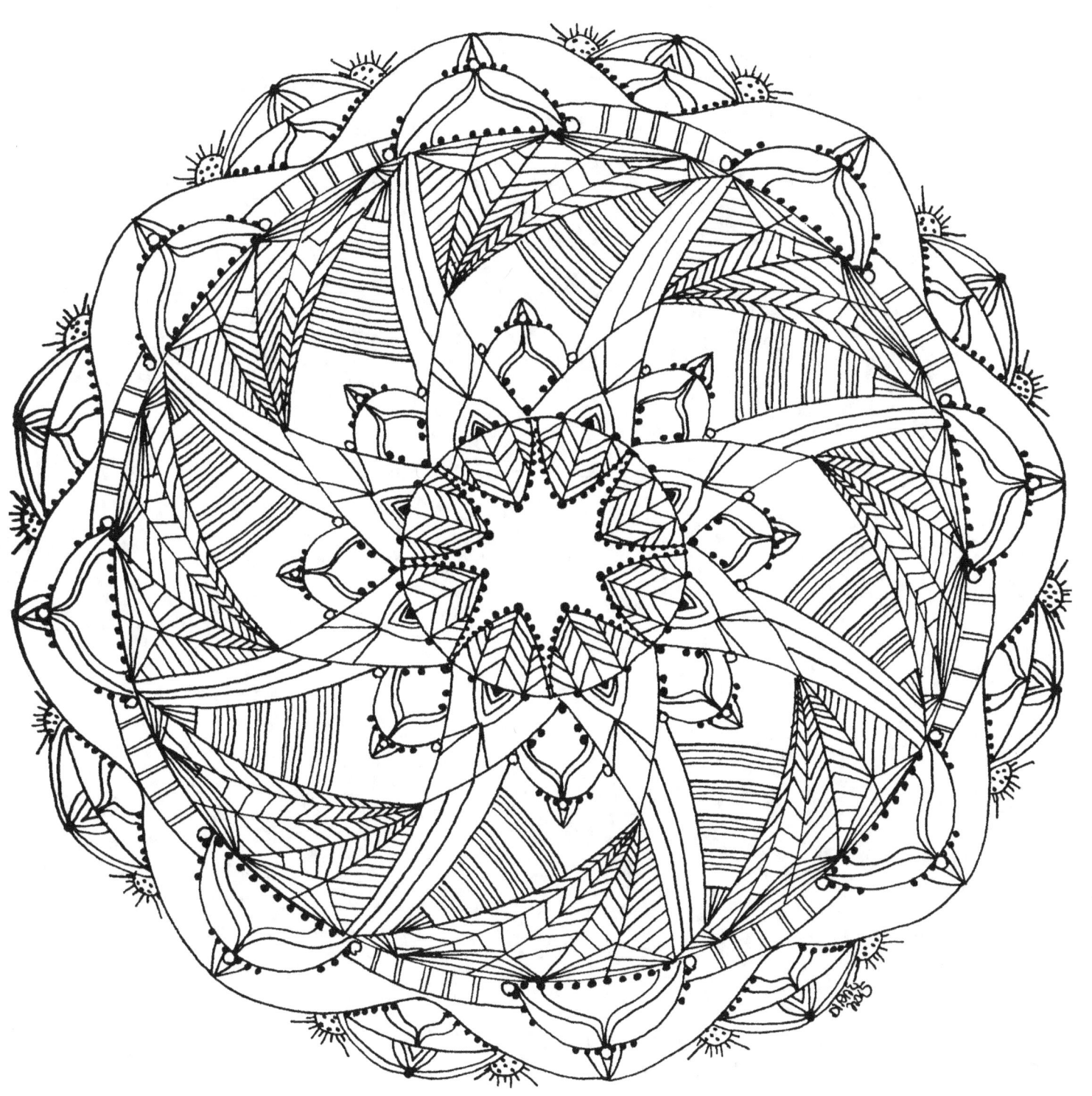

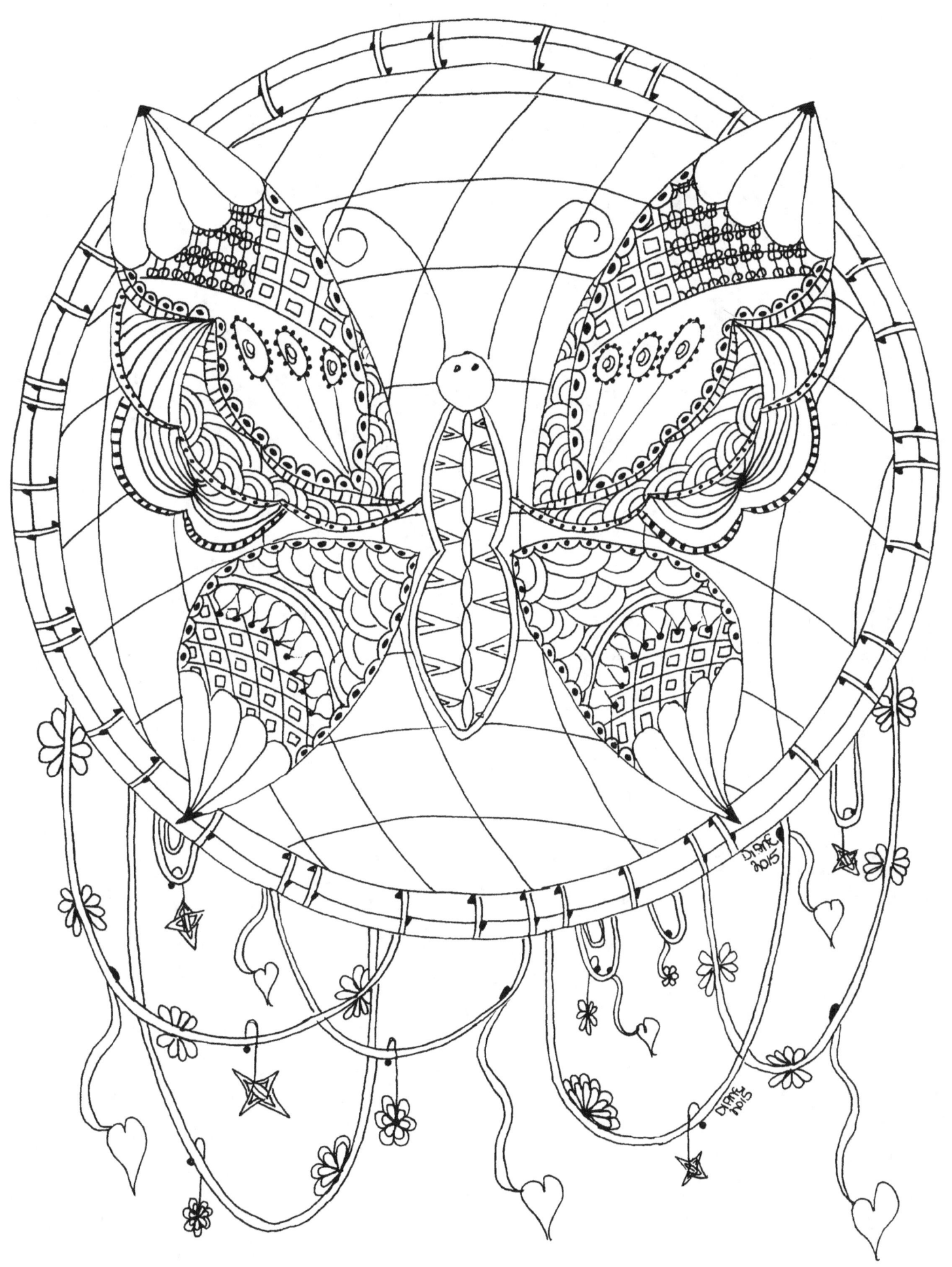

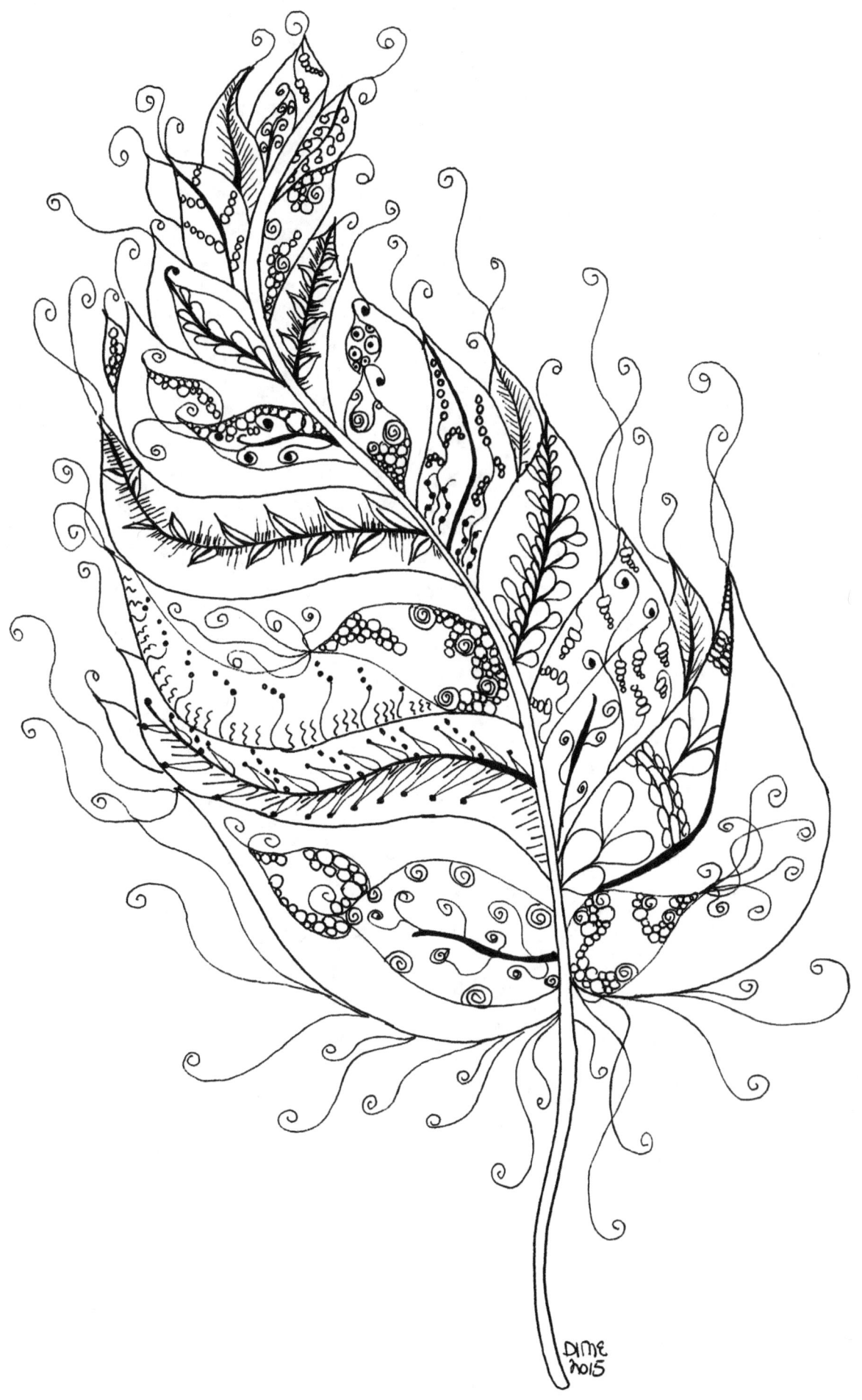

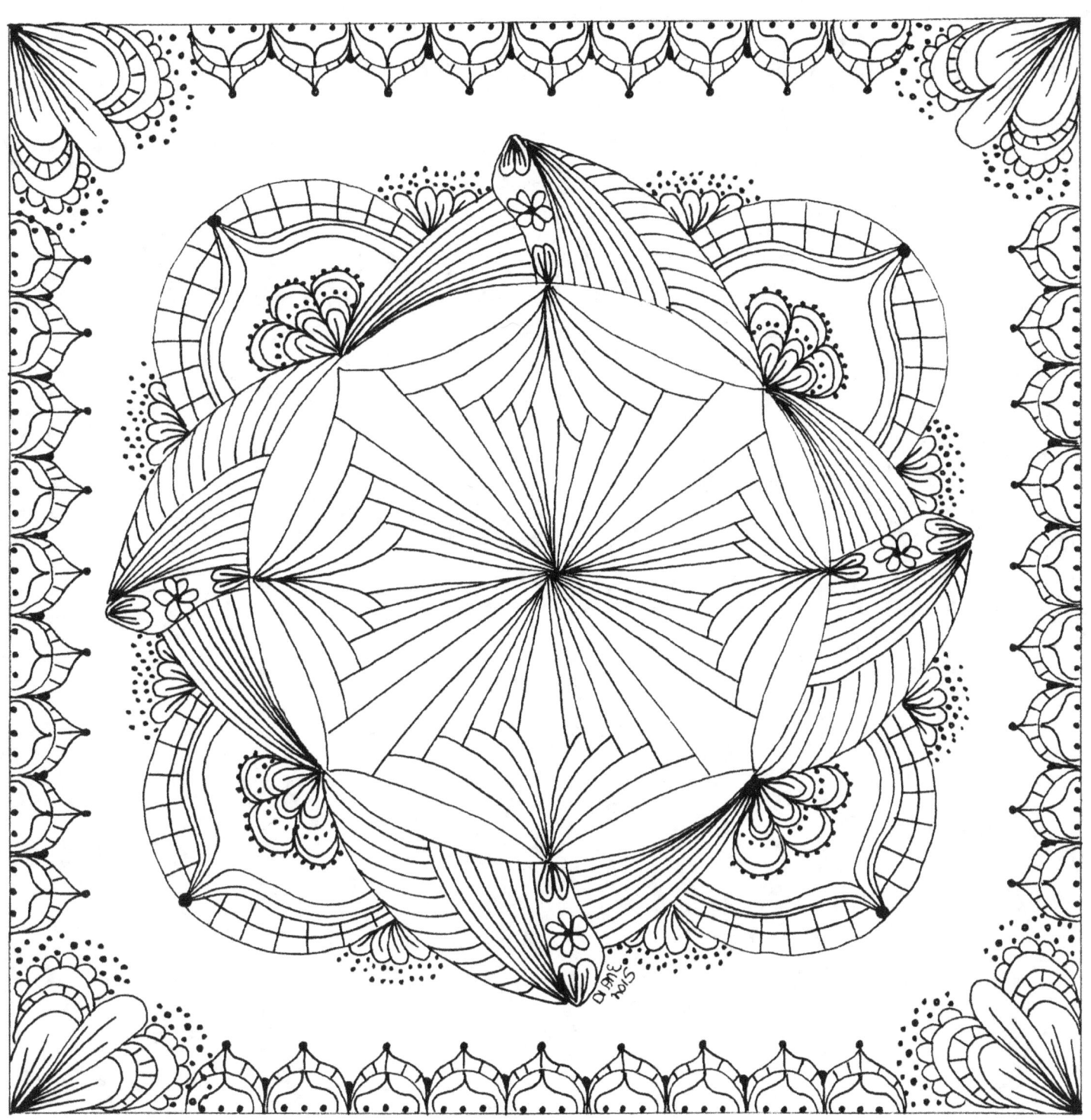

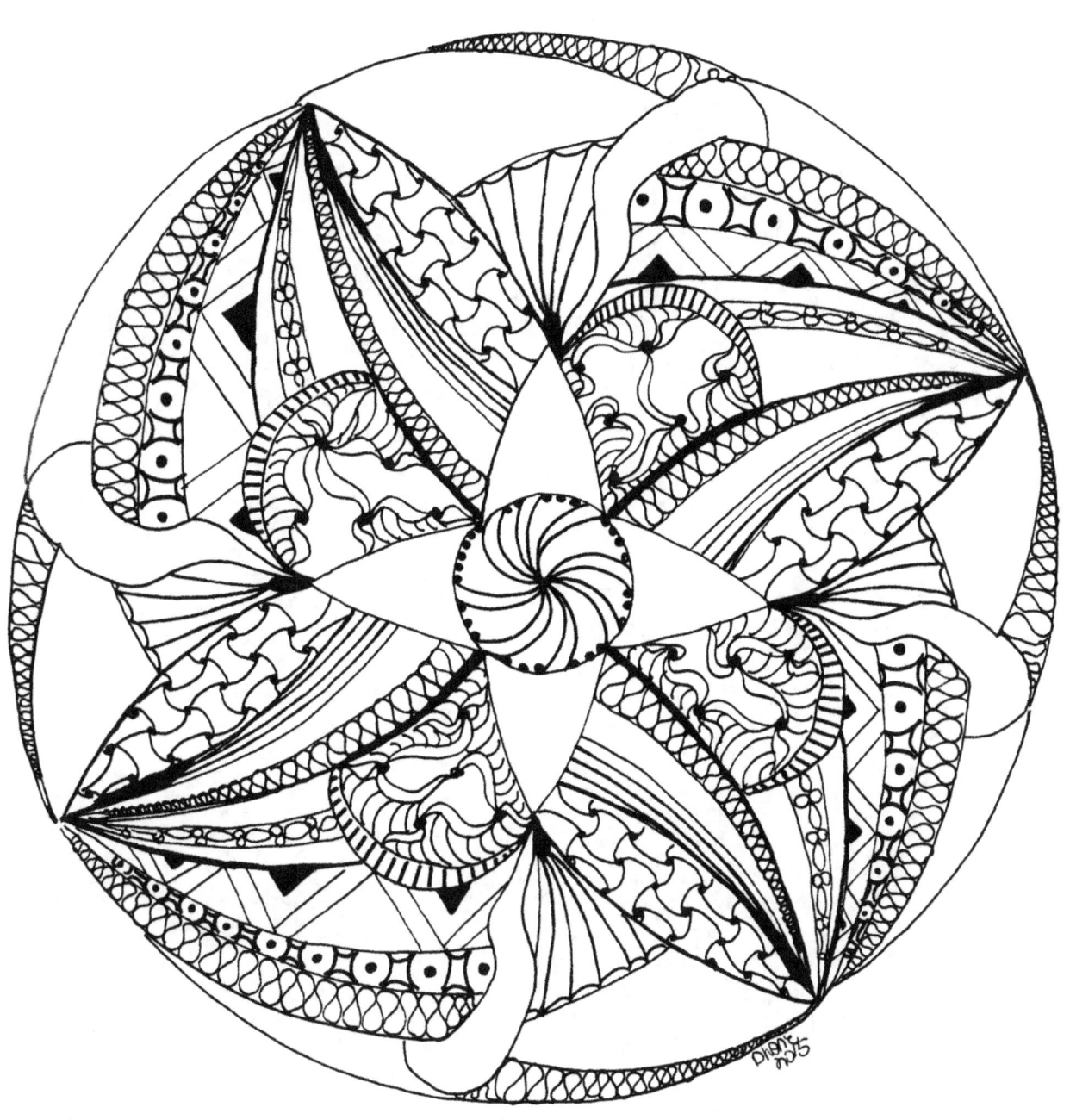

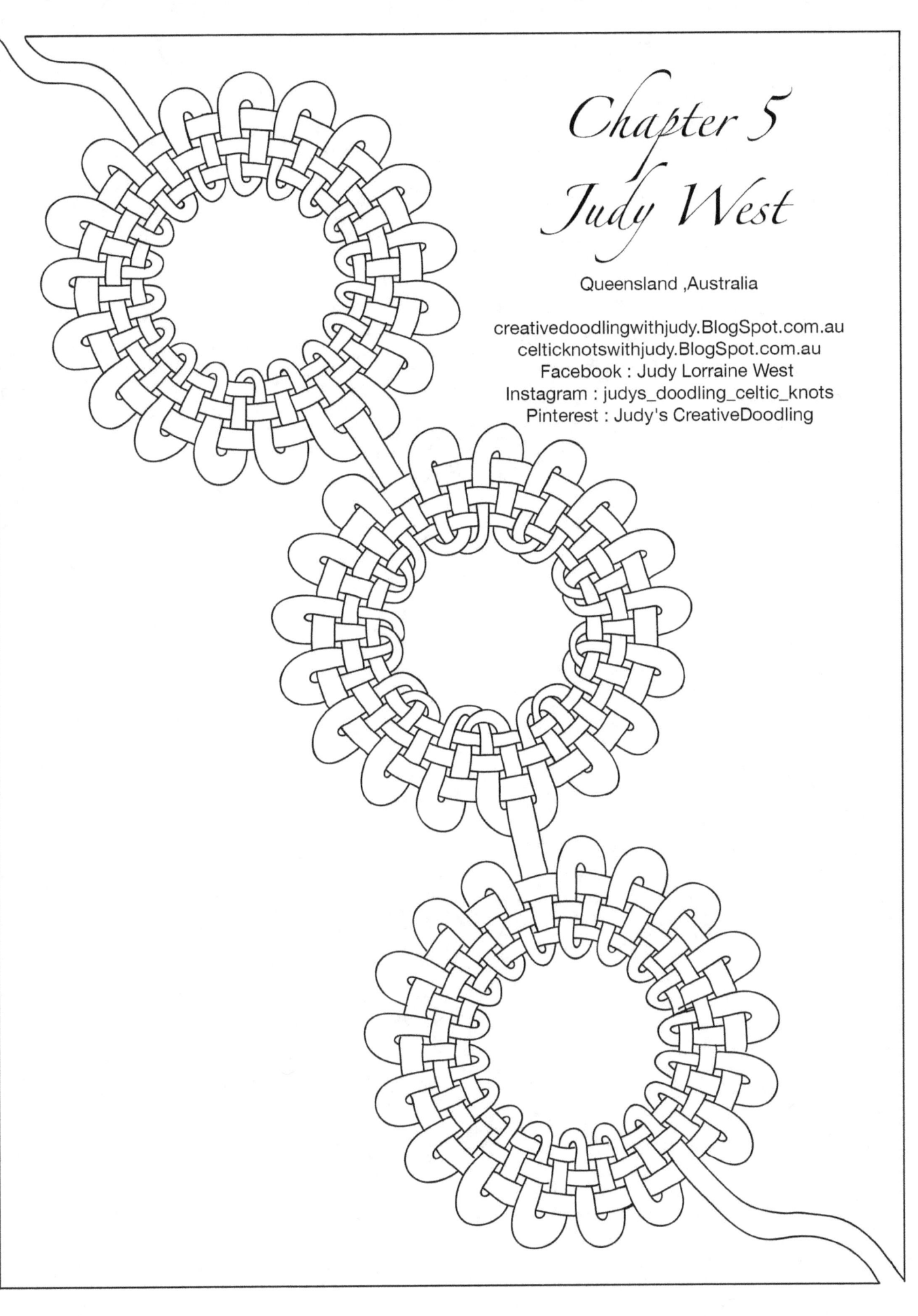

Chapter 5
Judy West

Queensland, Australia

creativedoodlingwithjudy.BlogSpot.com.au
celticknotswithjudy.BlogSpot.com.au
Facebook : Judy Lorraine West
Instagram : judys_doodling_celtic_knots
Pinterest : Judy's CreativeDoodling

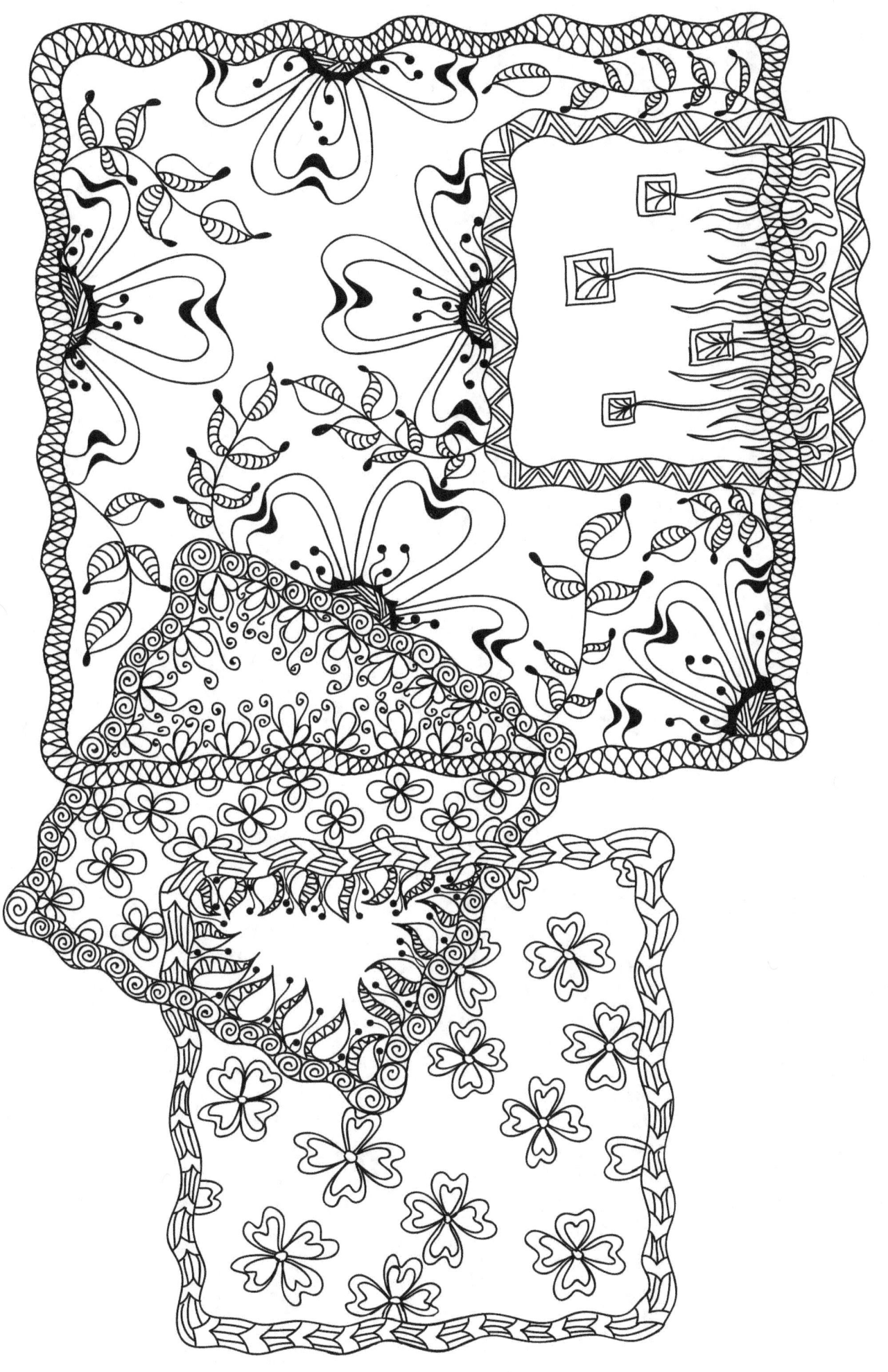

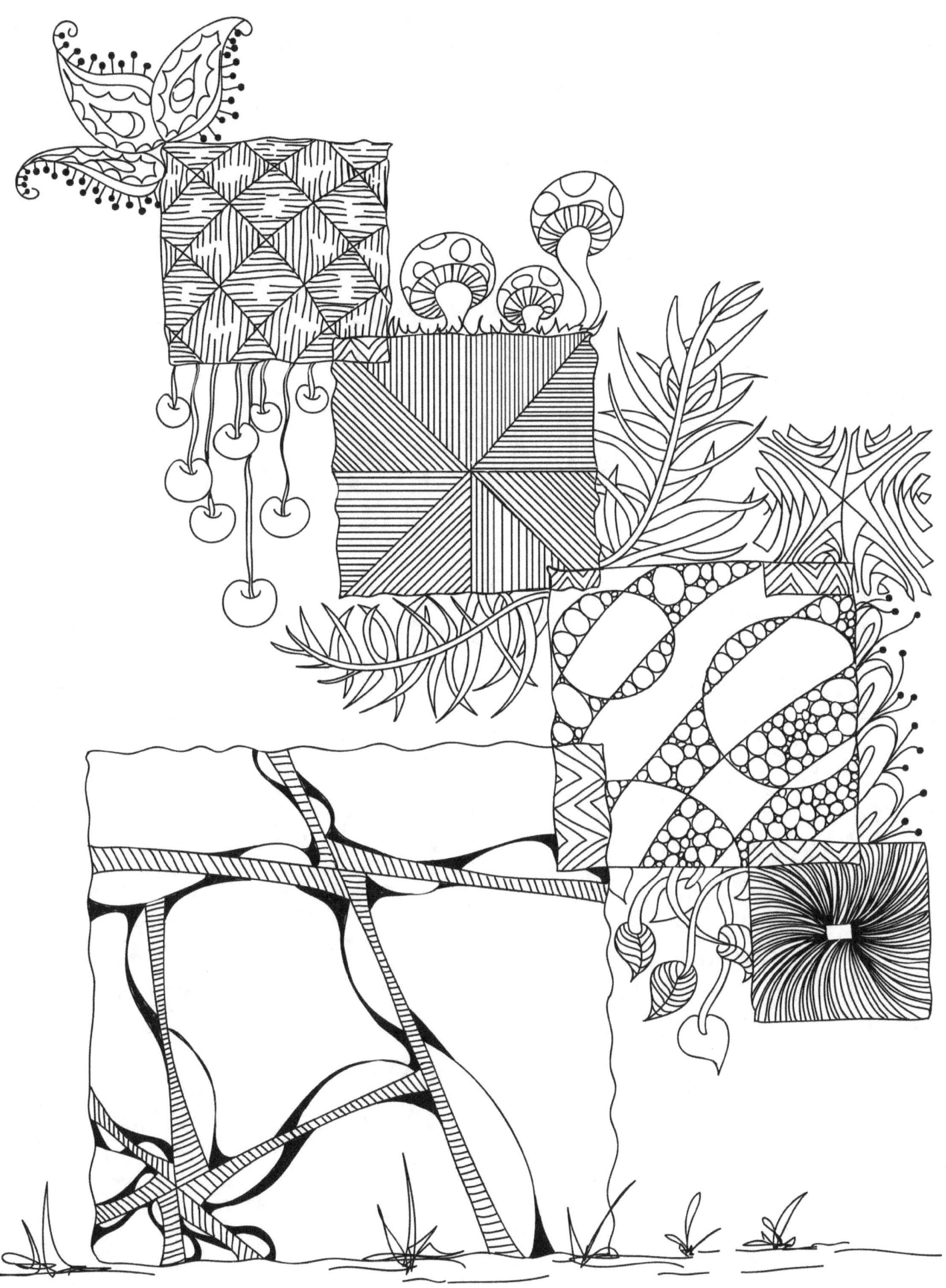

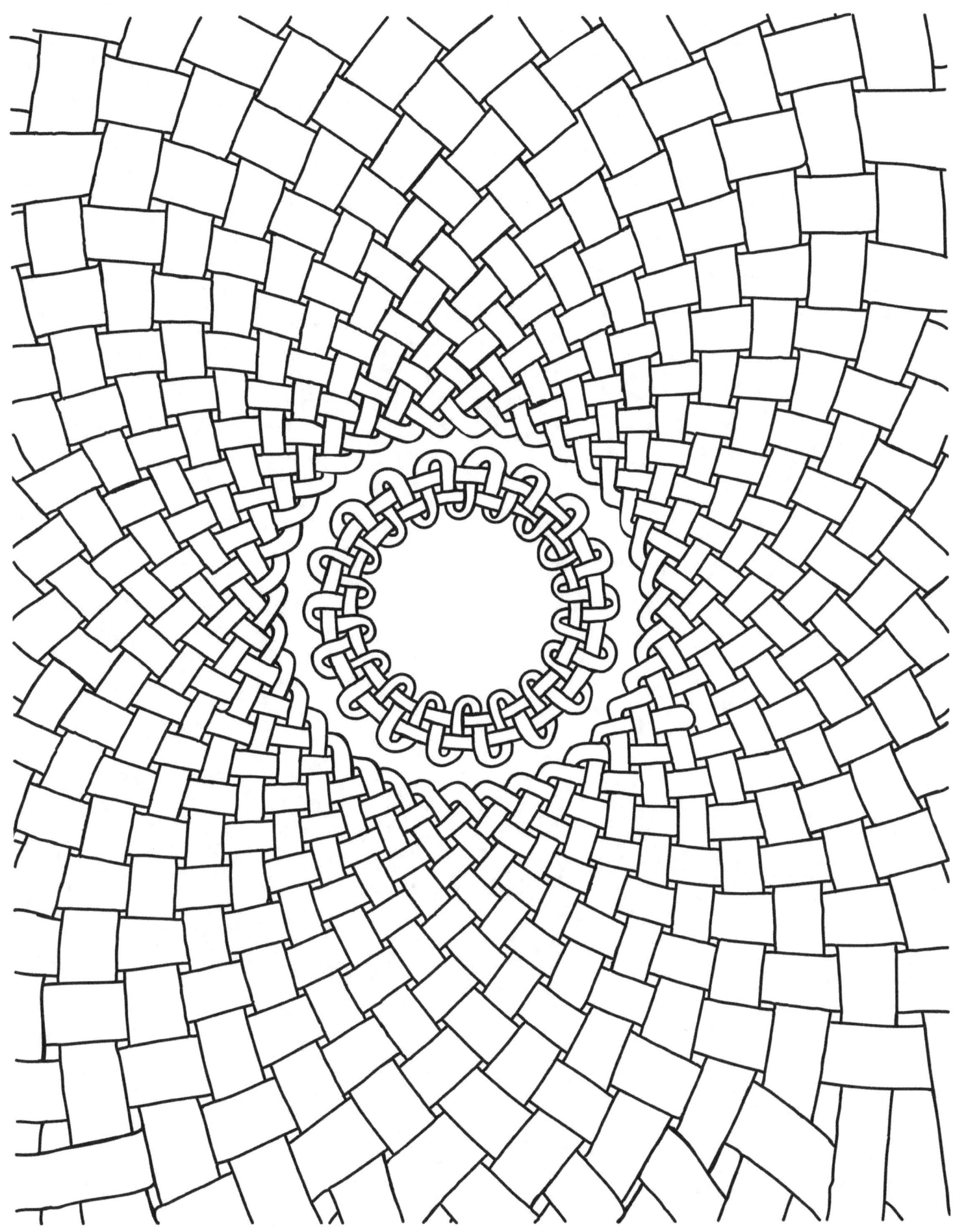

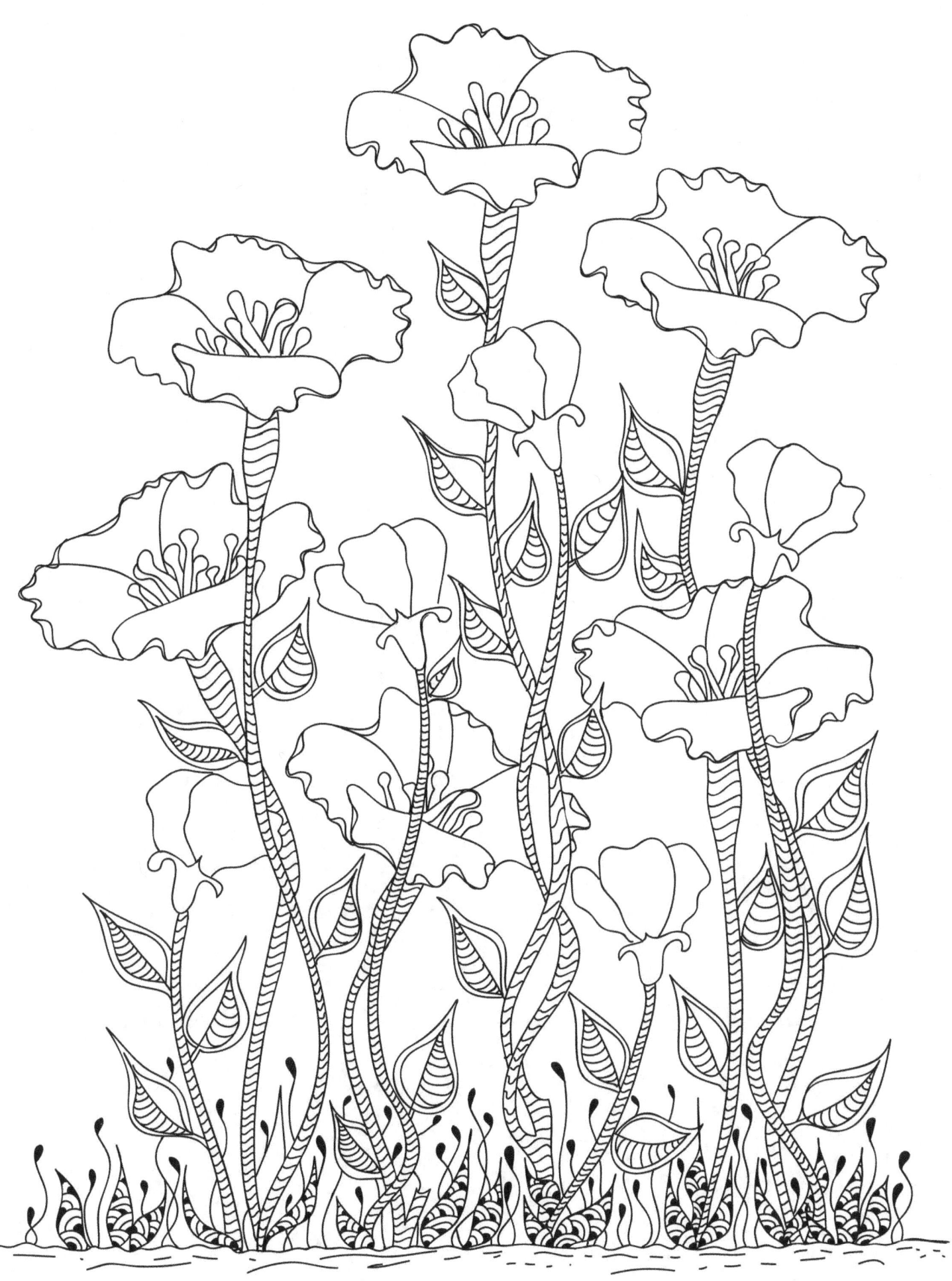

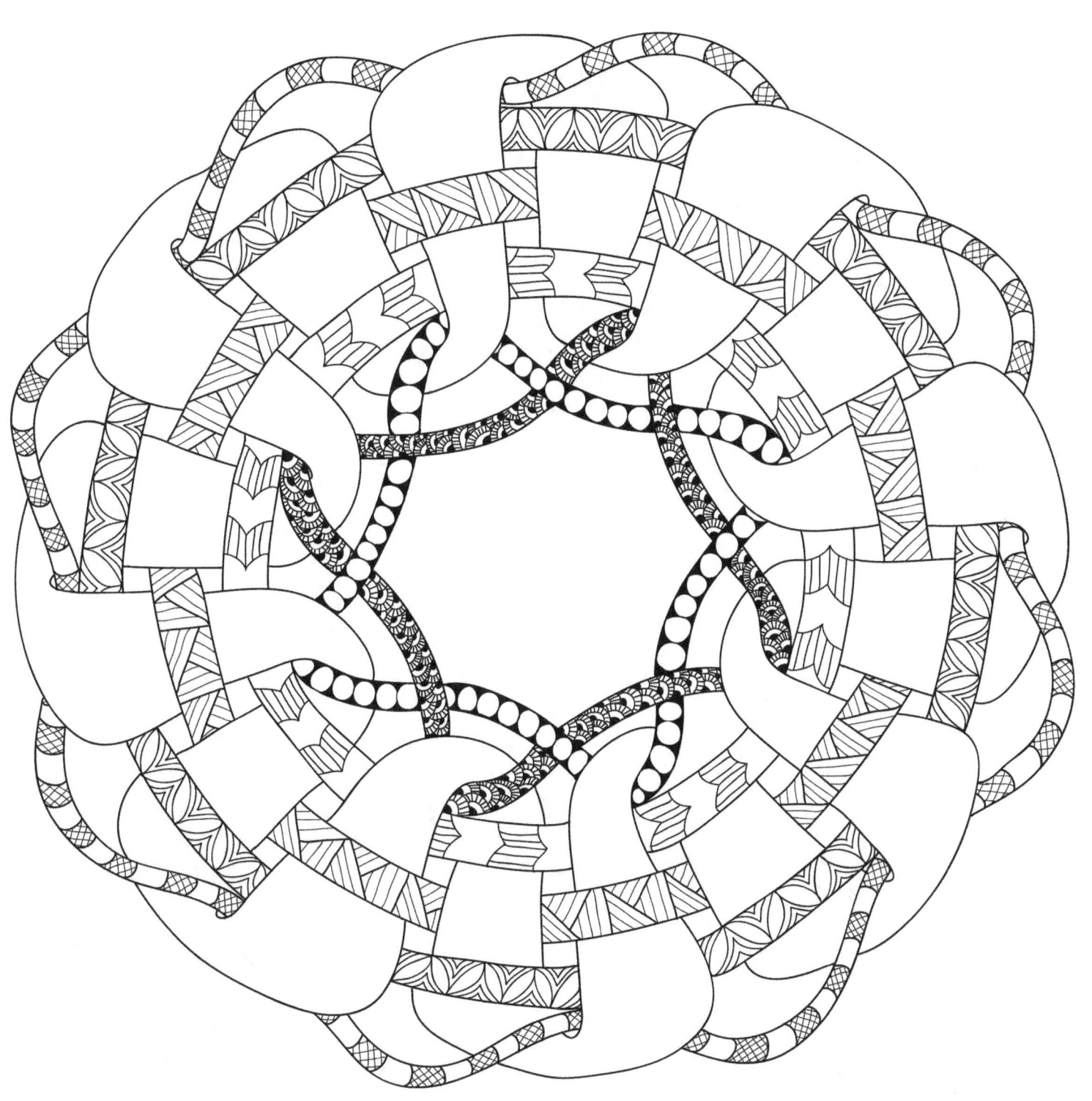

Chapter 6
Arqui

Philippines
Facebook : Arqui-Doodle

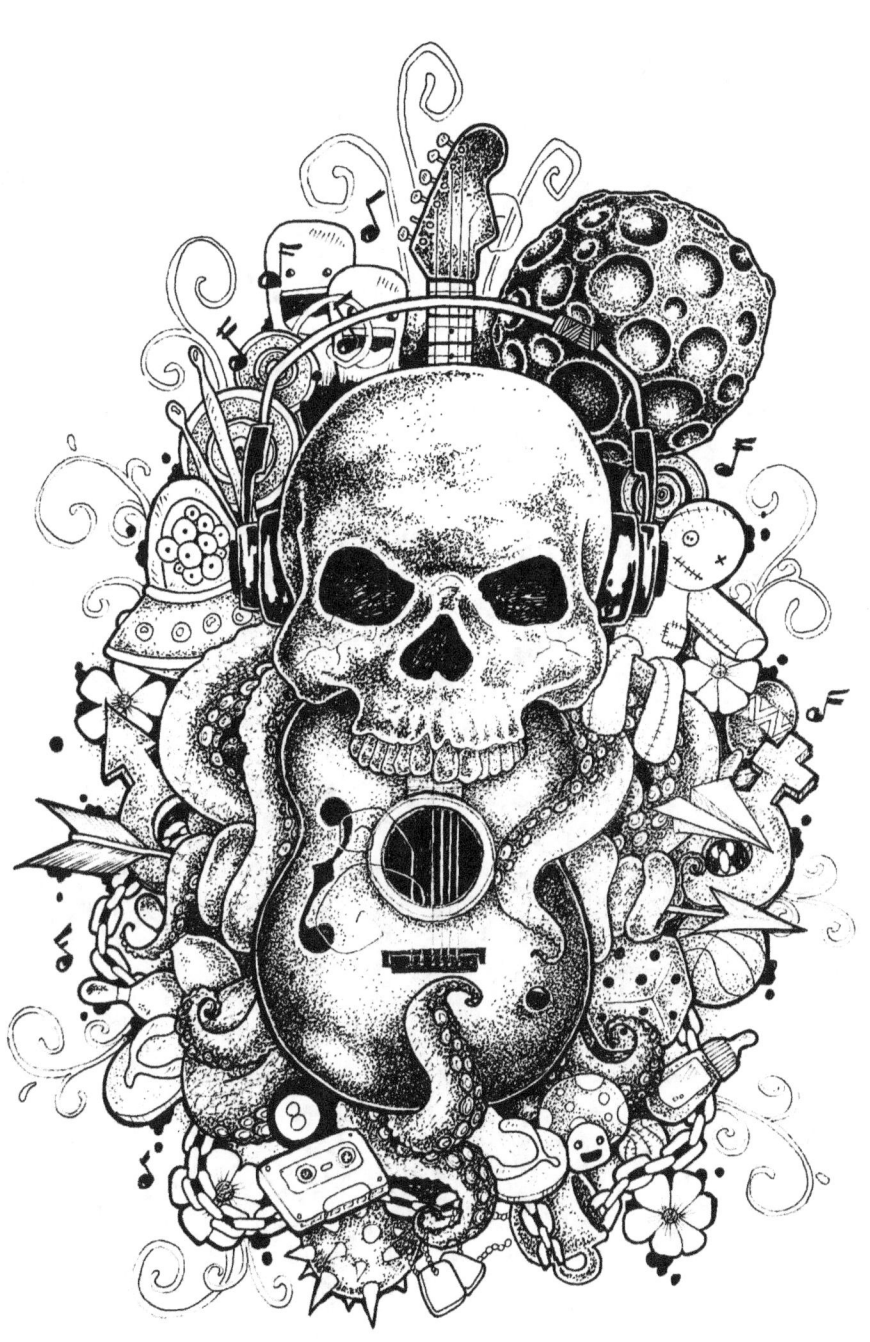

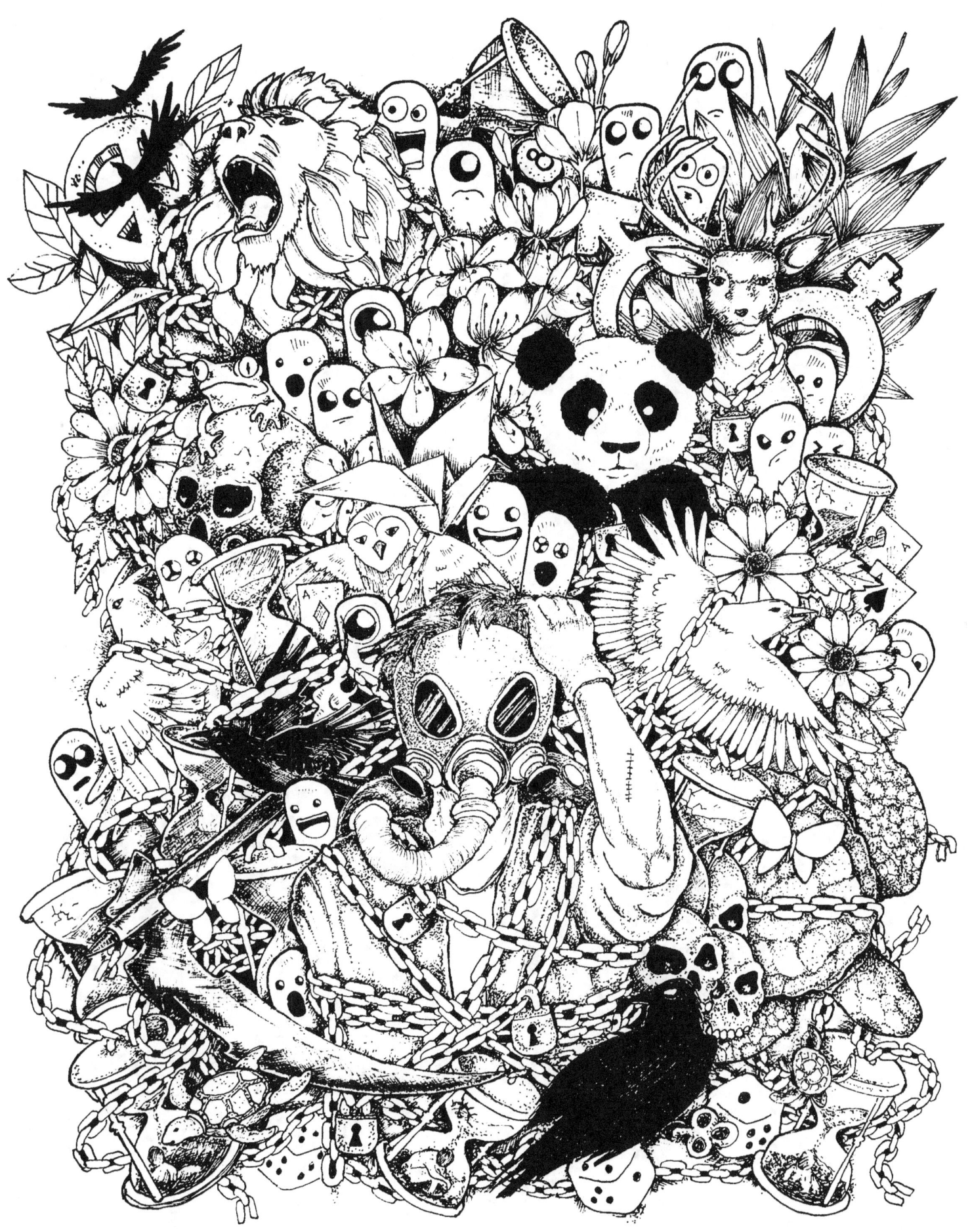

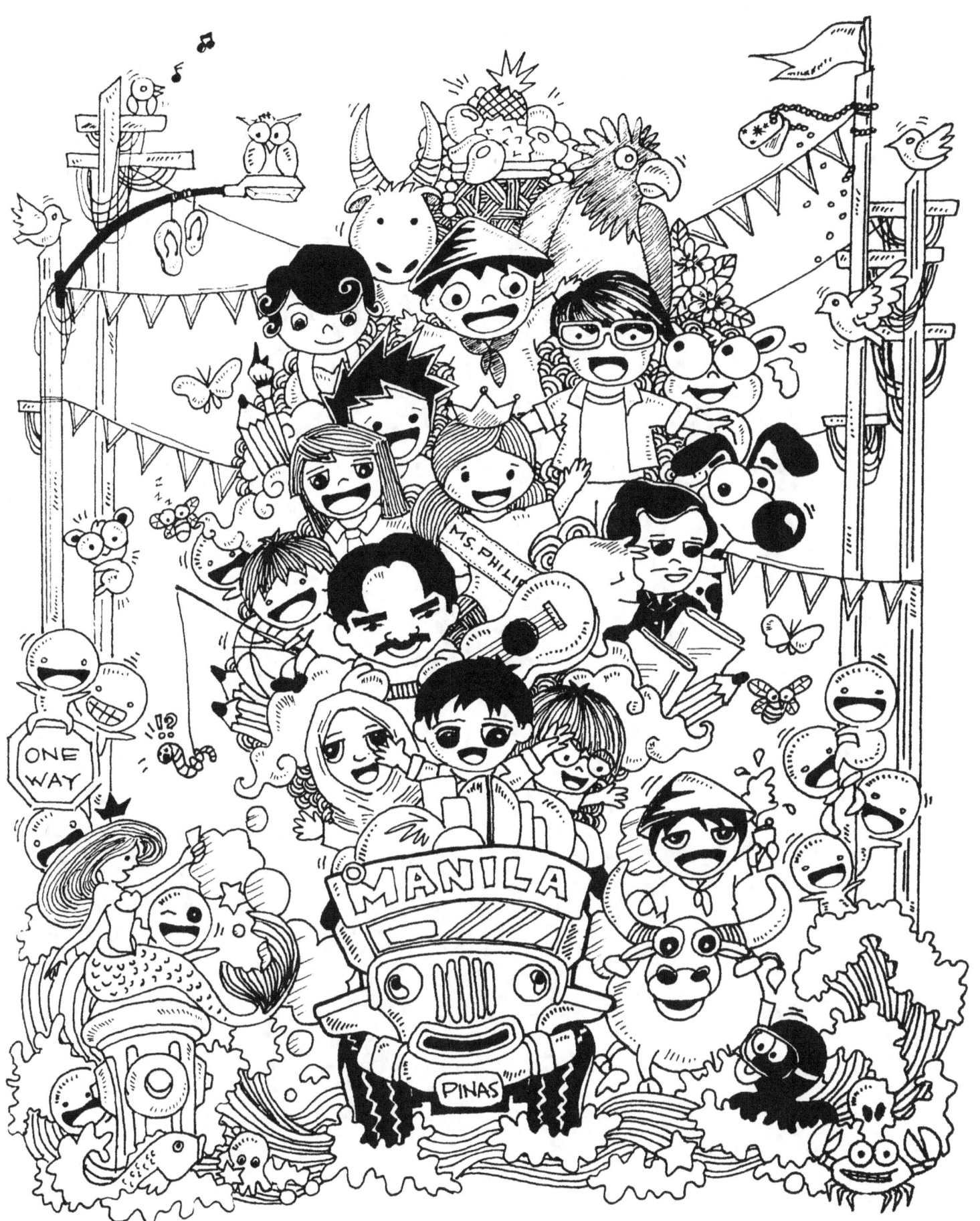

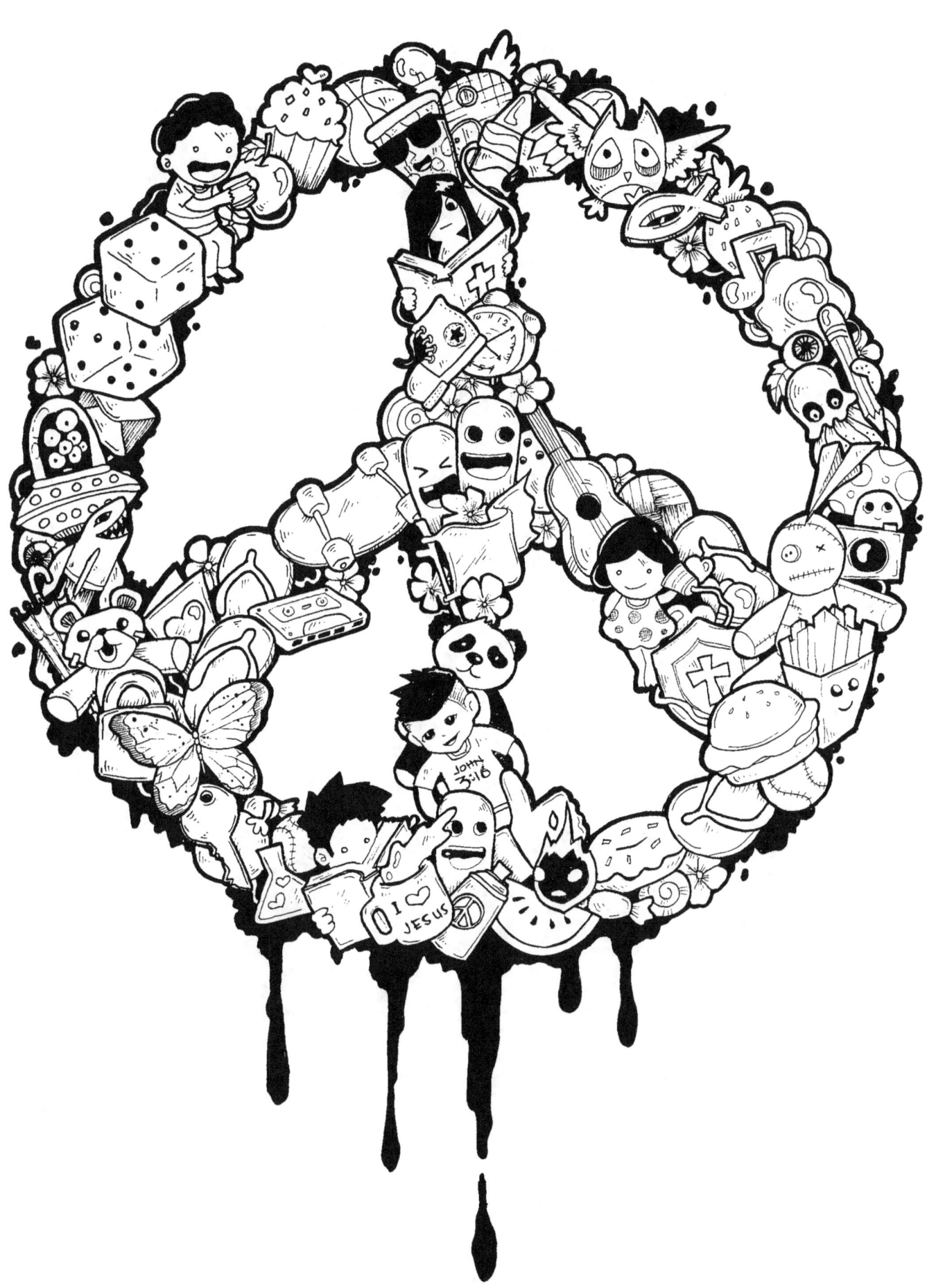

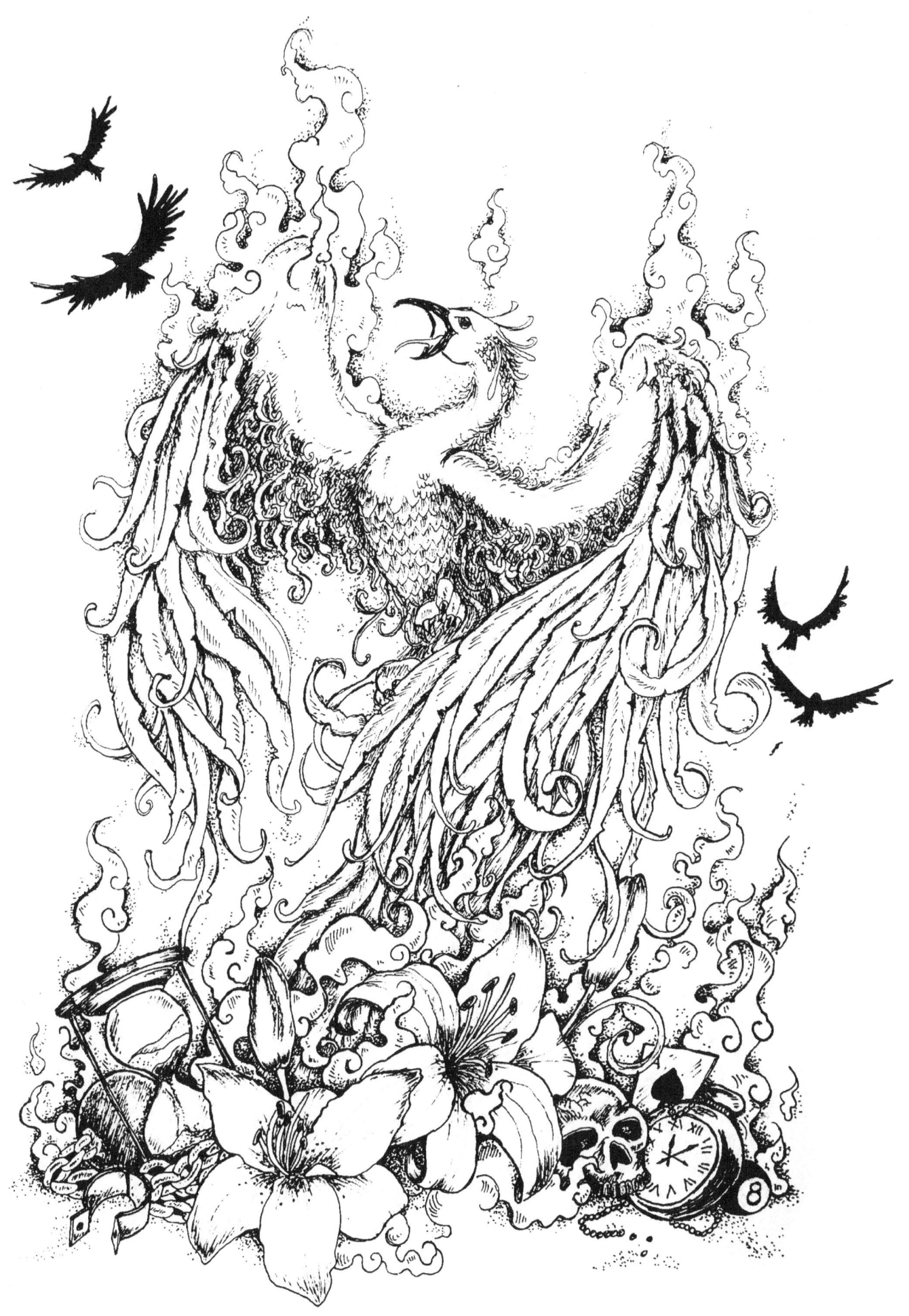

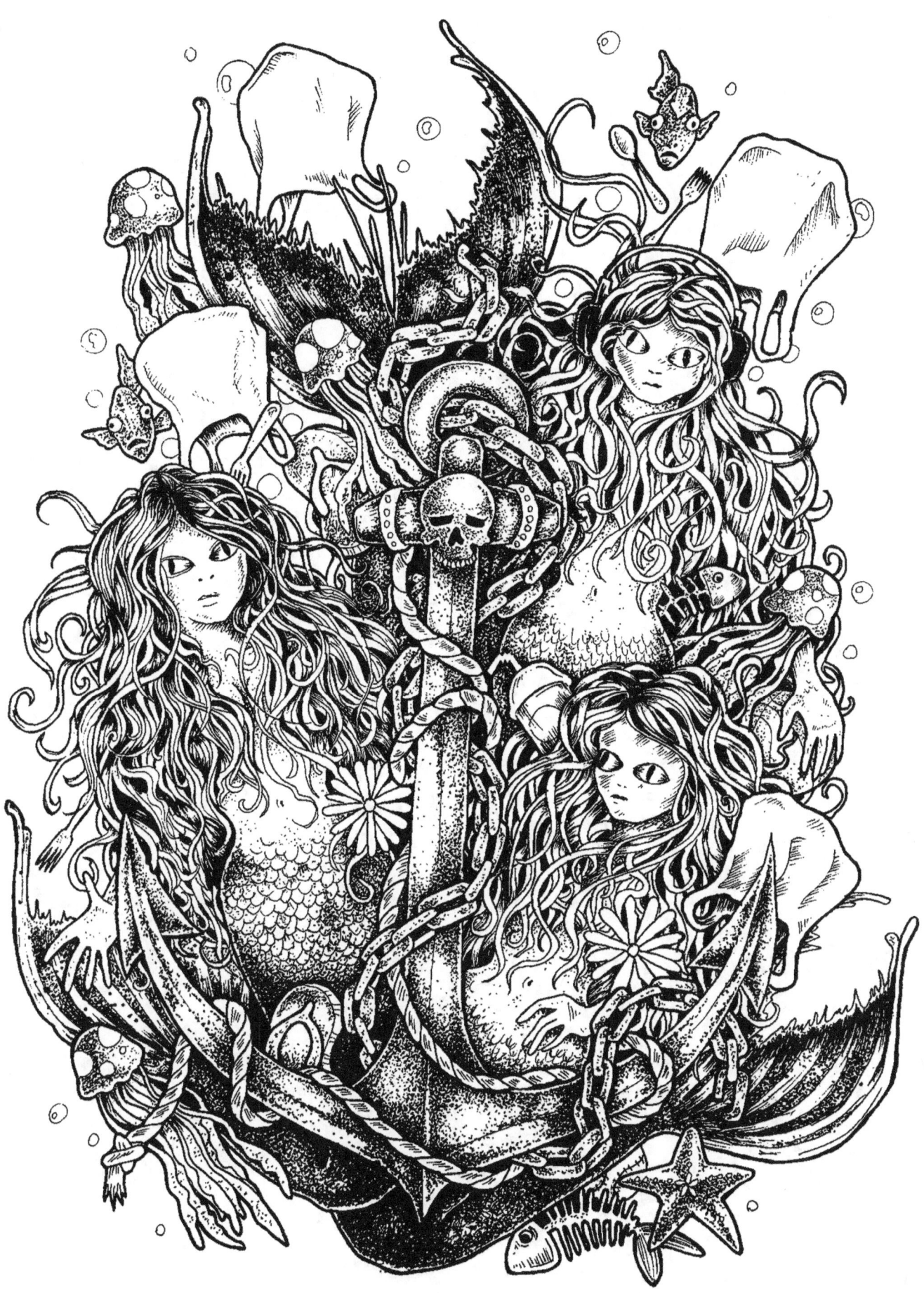

Chapter 7
Shelly Eartha Simpson

Brazil

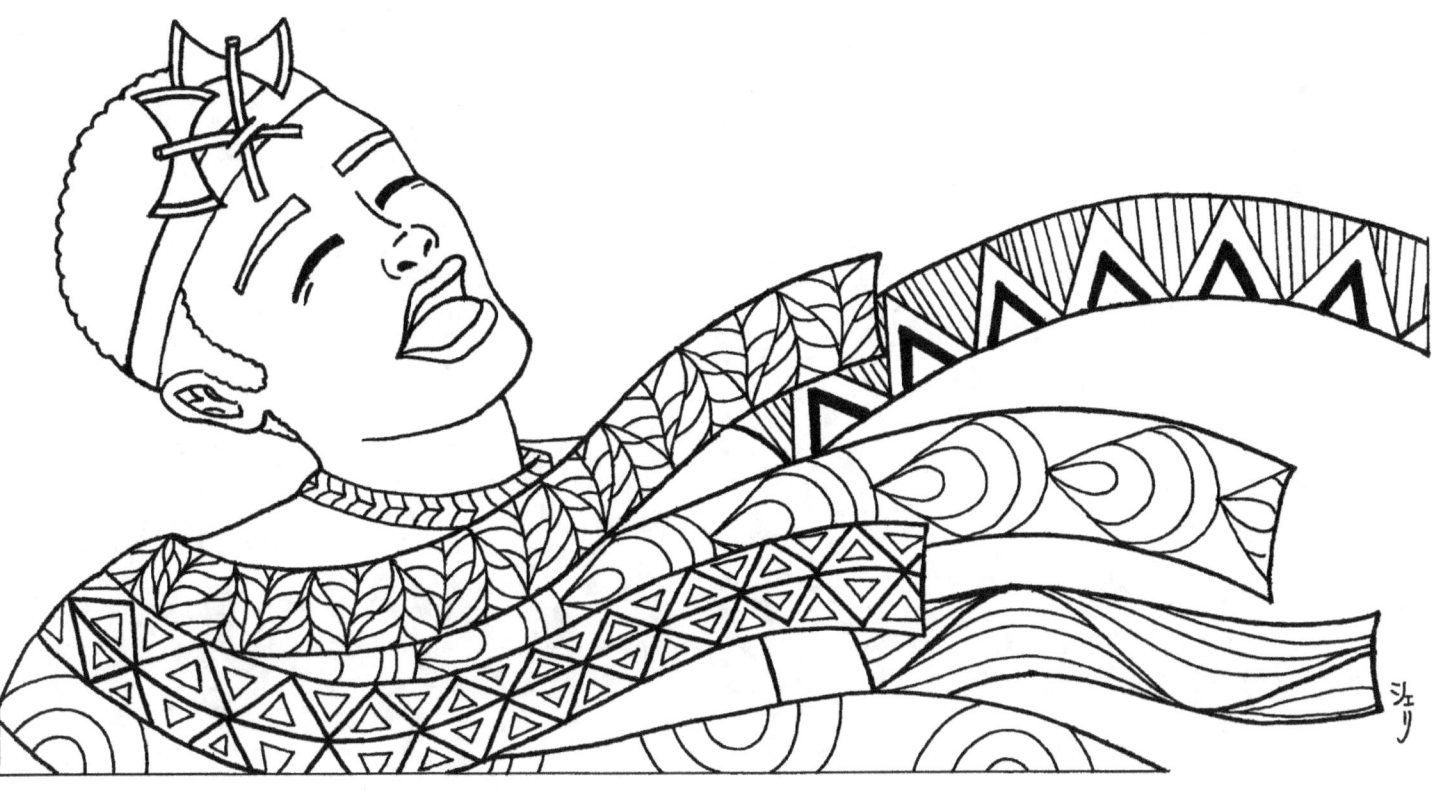

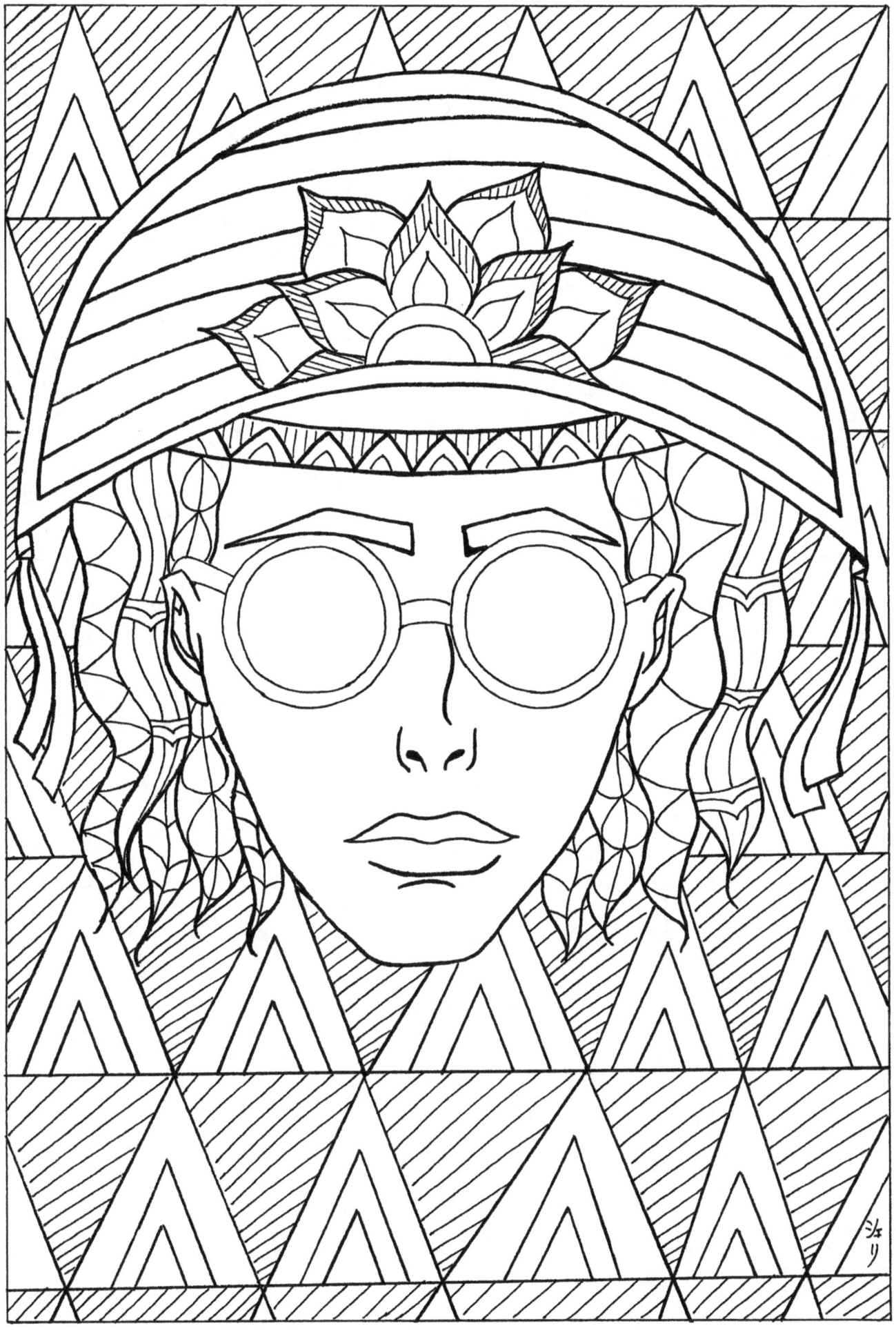

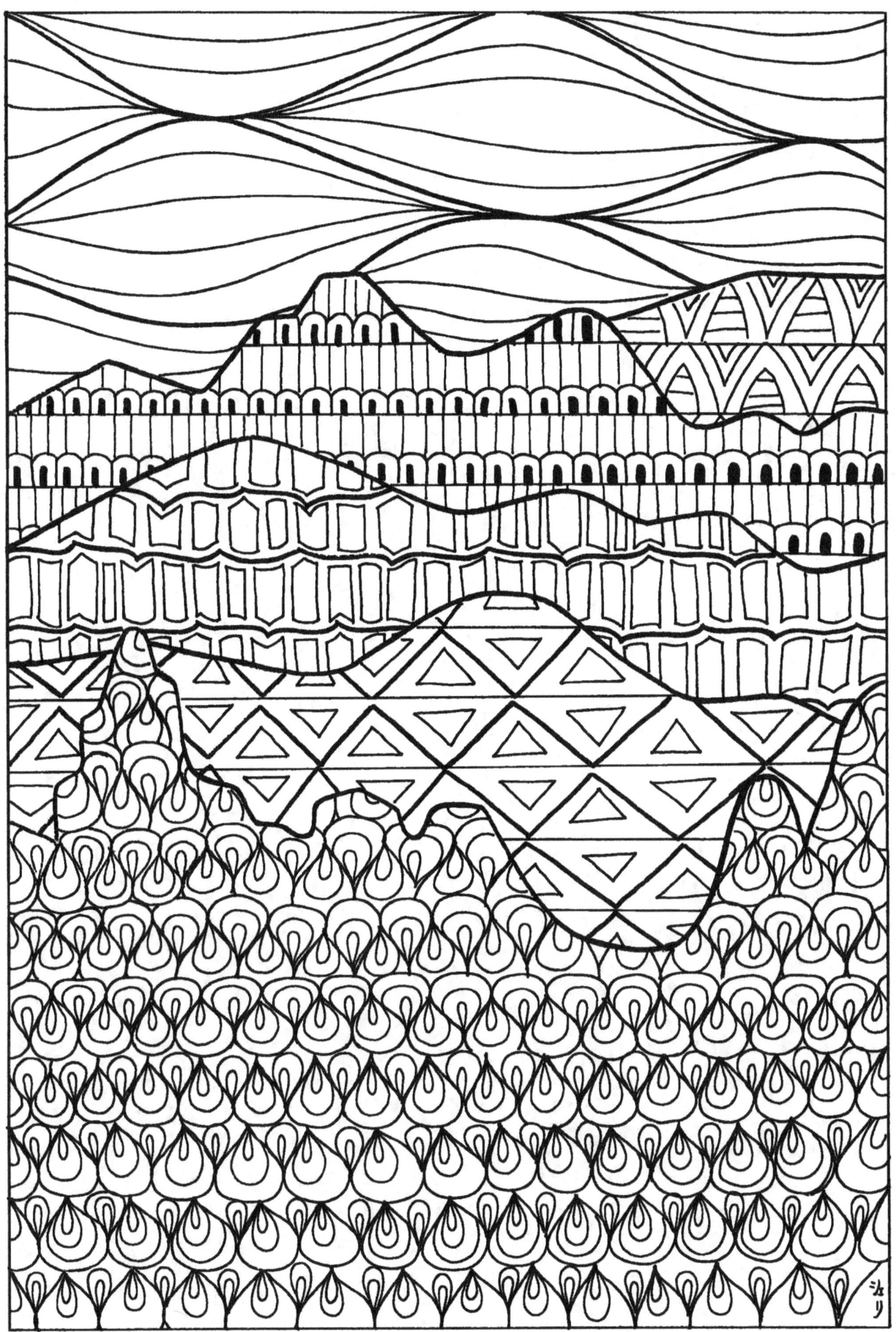

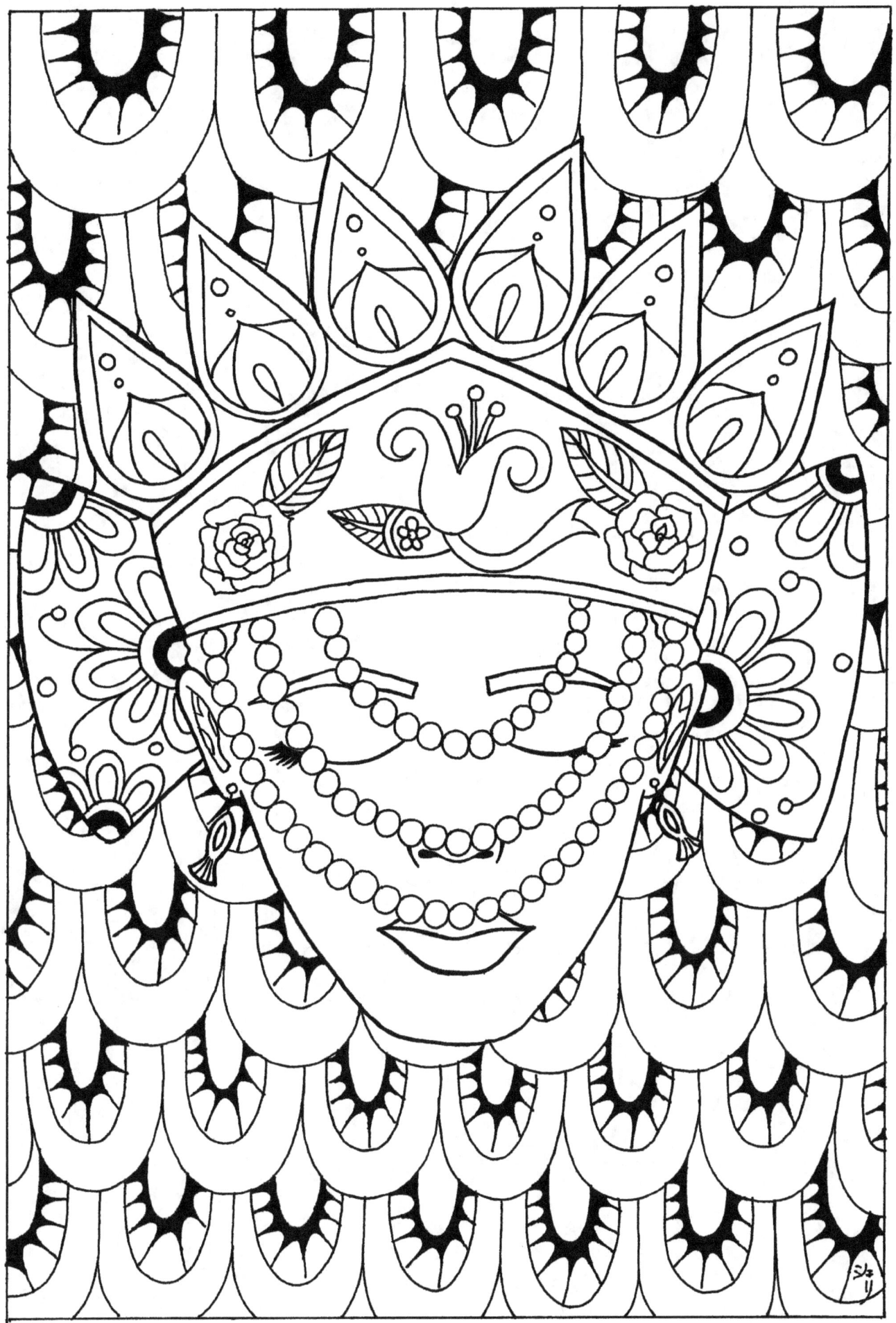

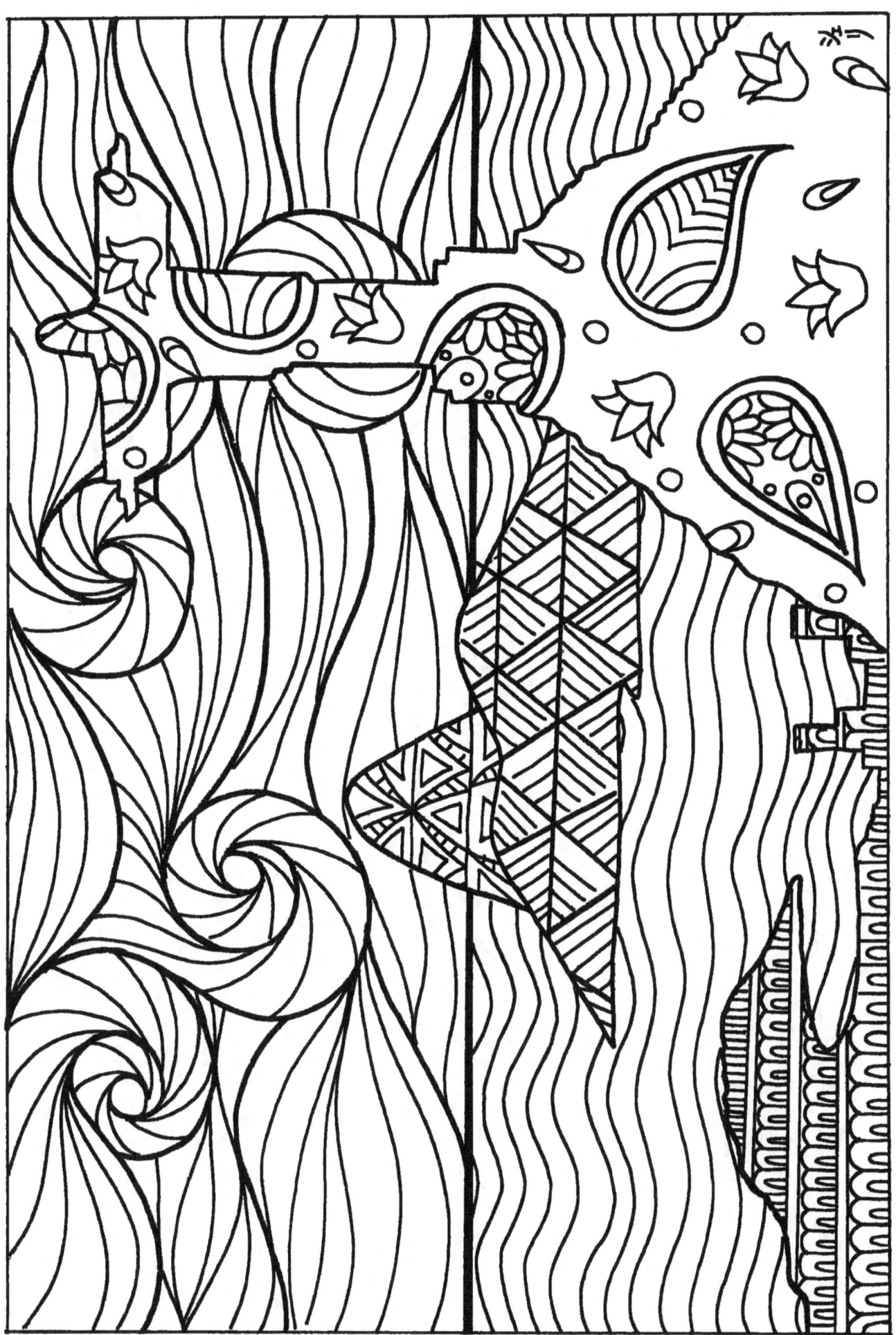

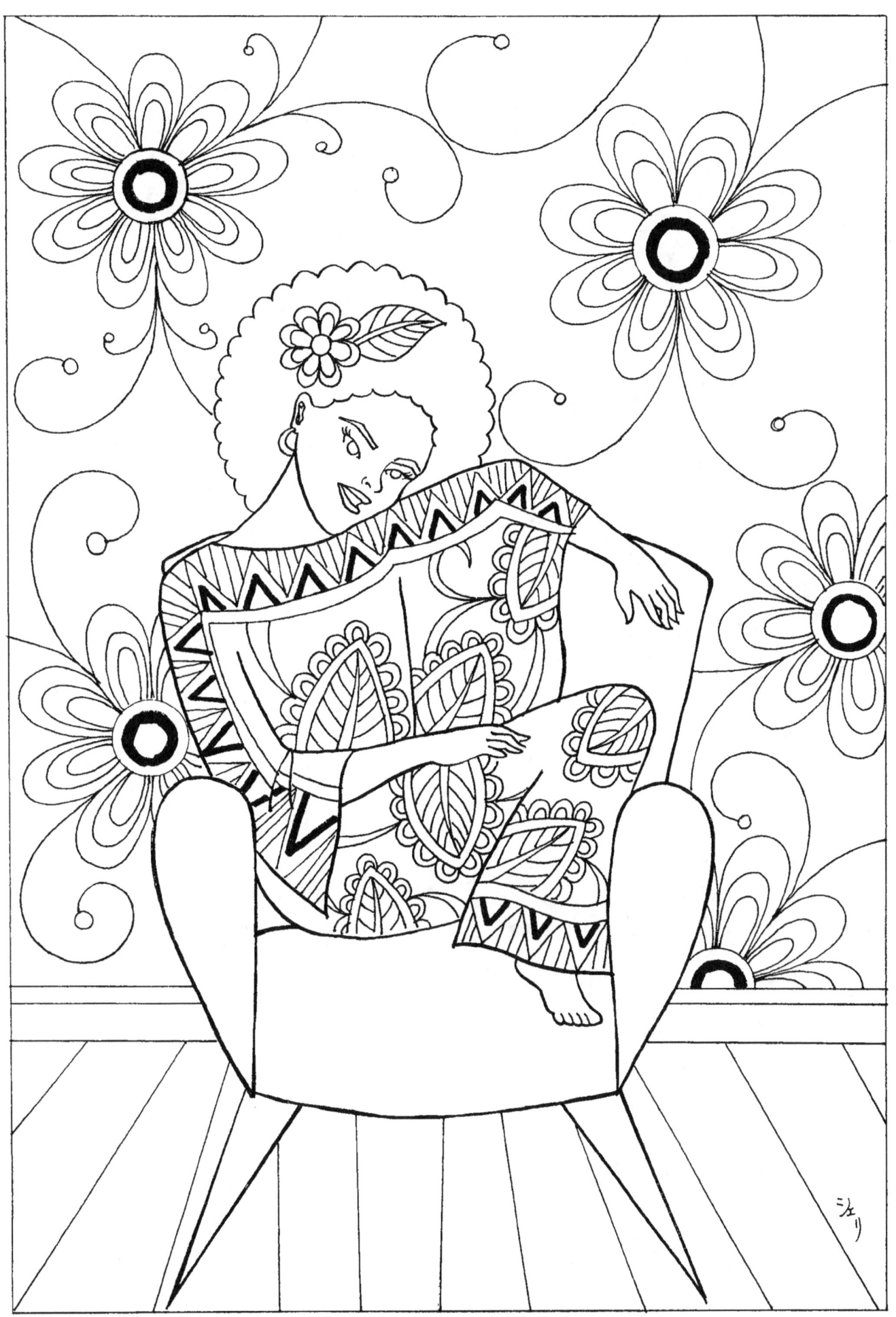

Chapter 8
Dawn Miller

USA

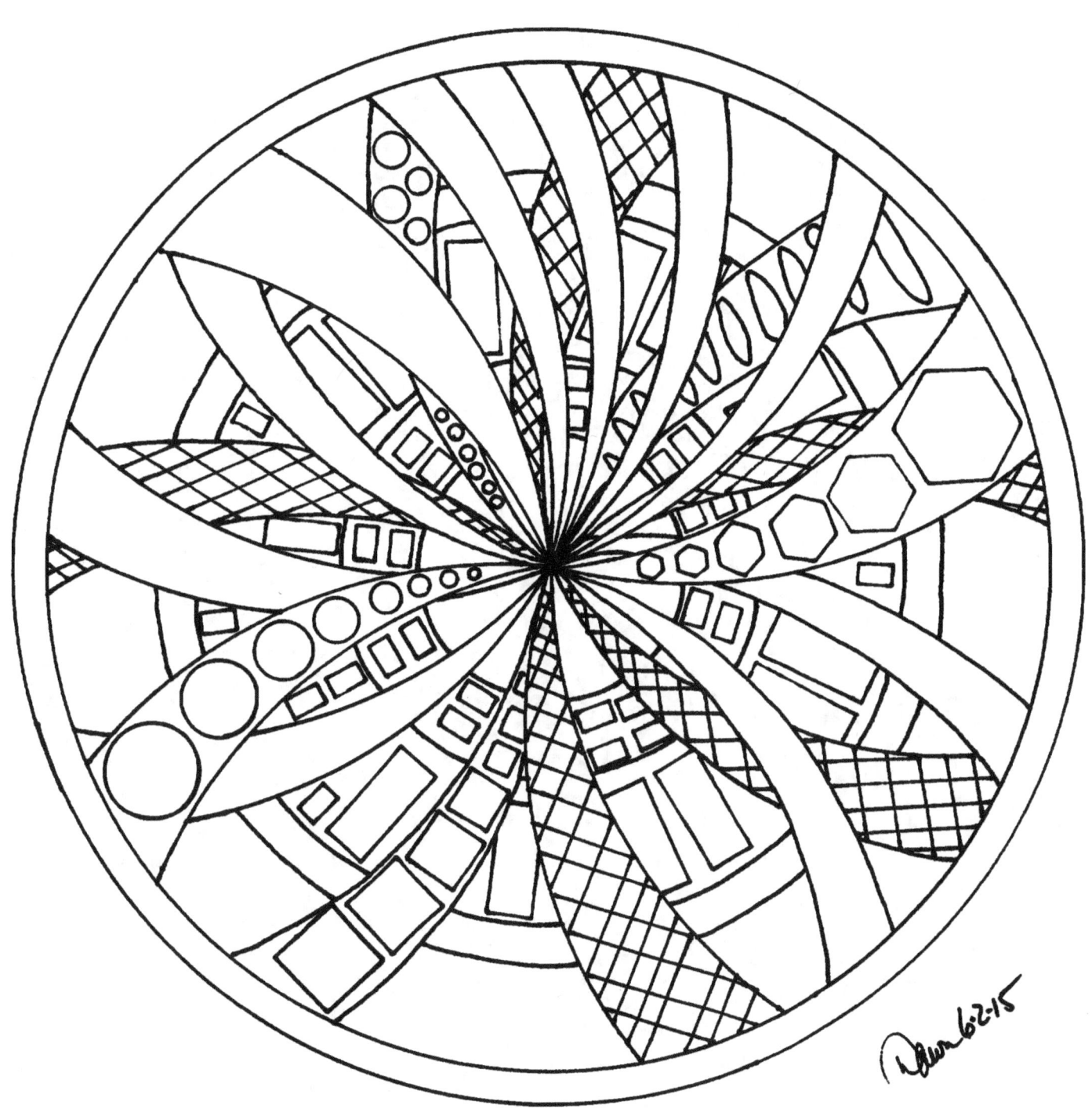

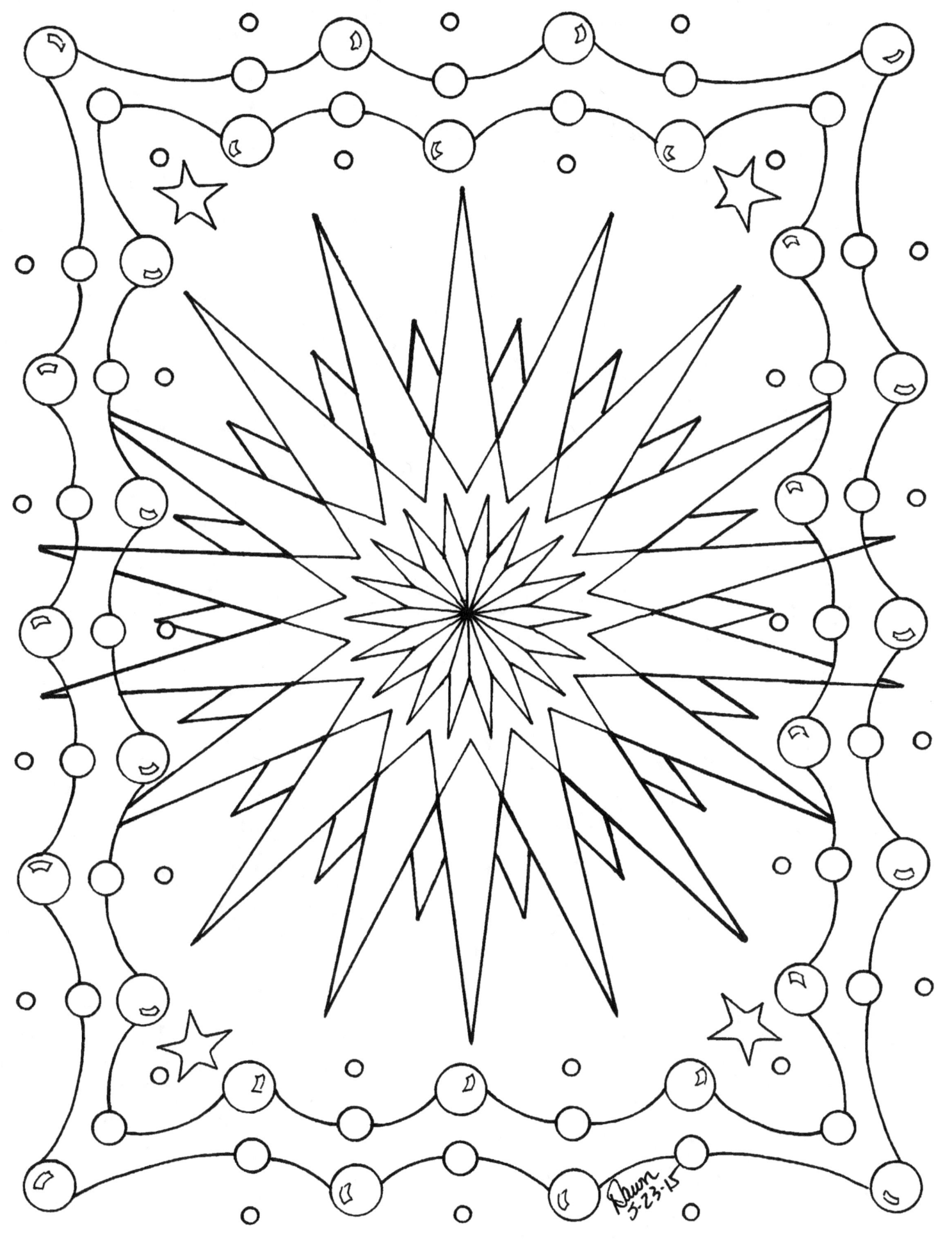

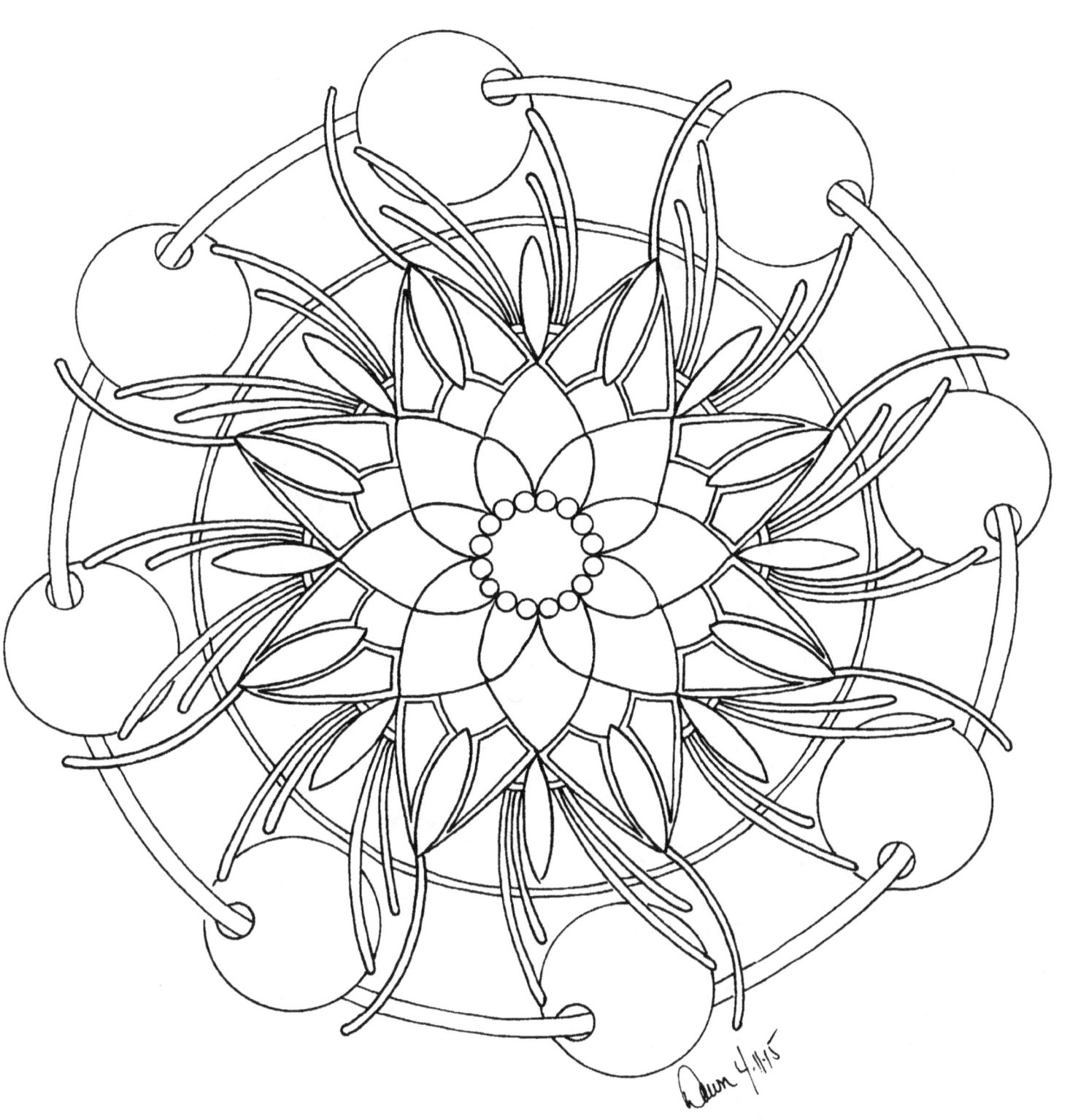

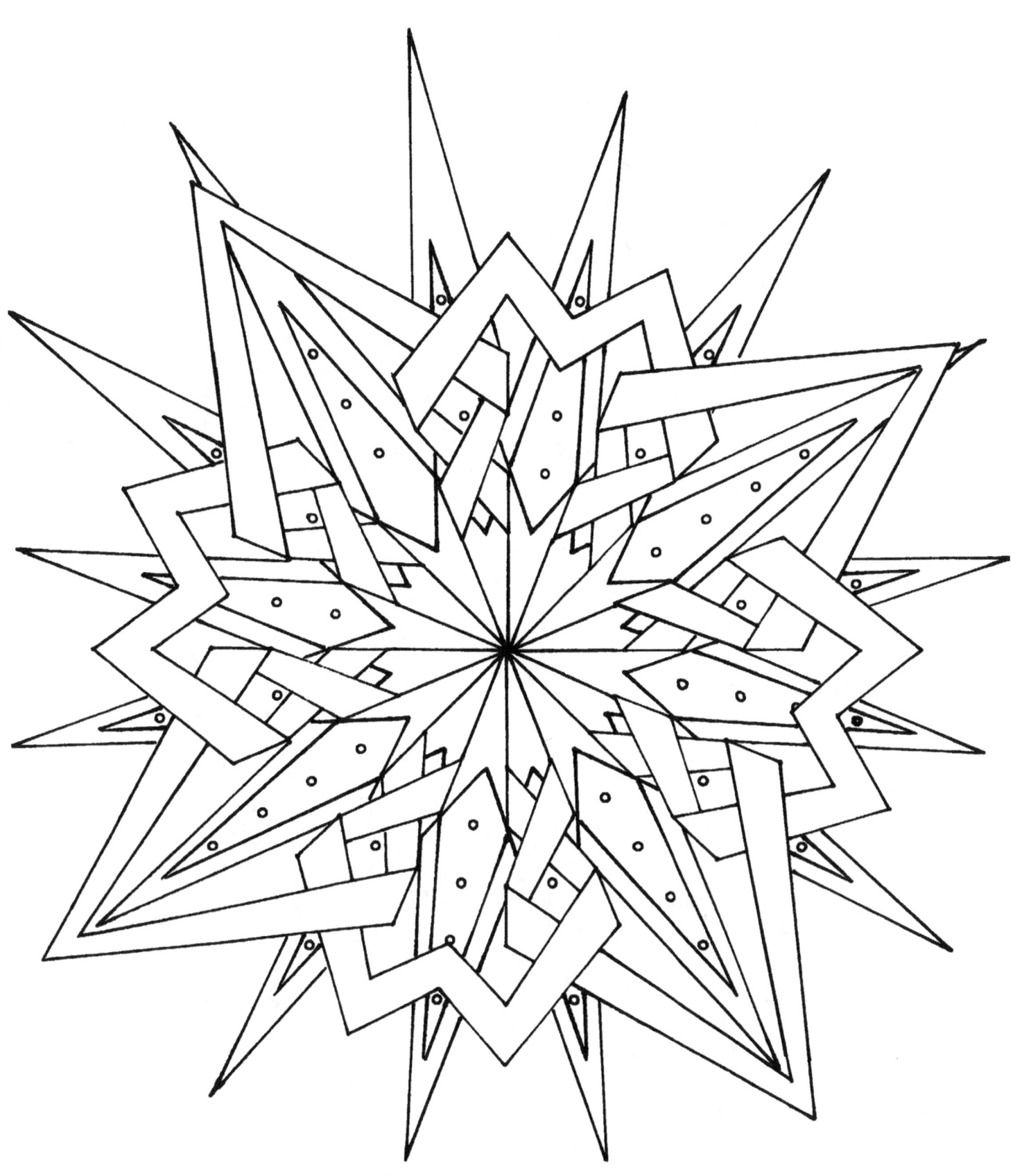

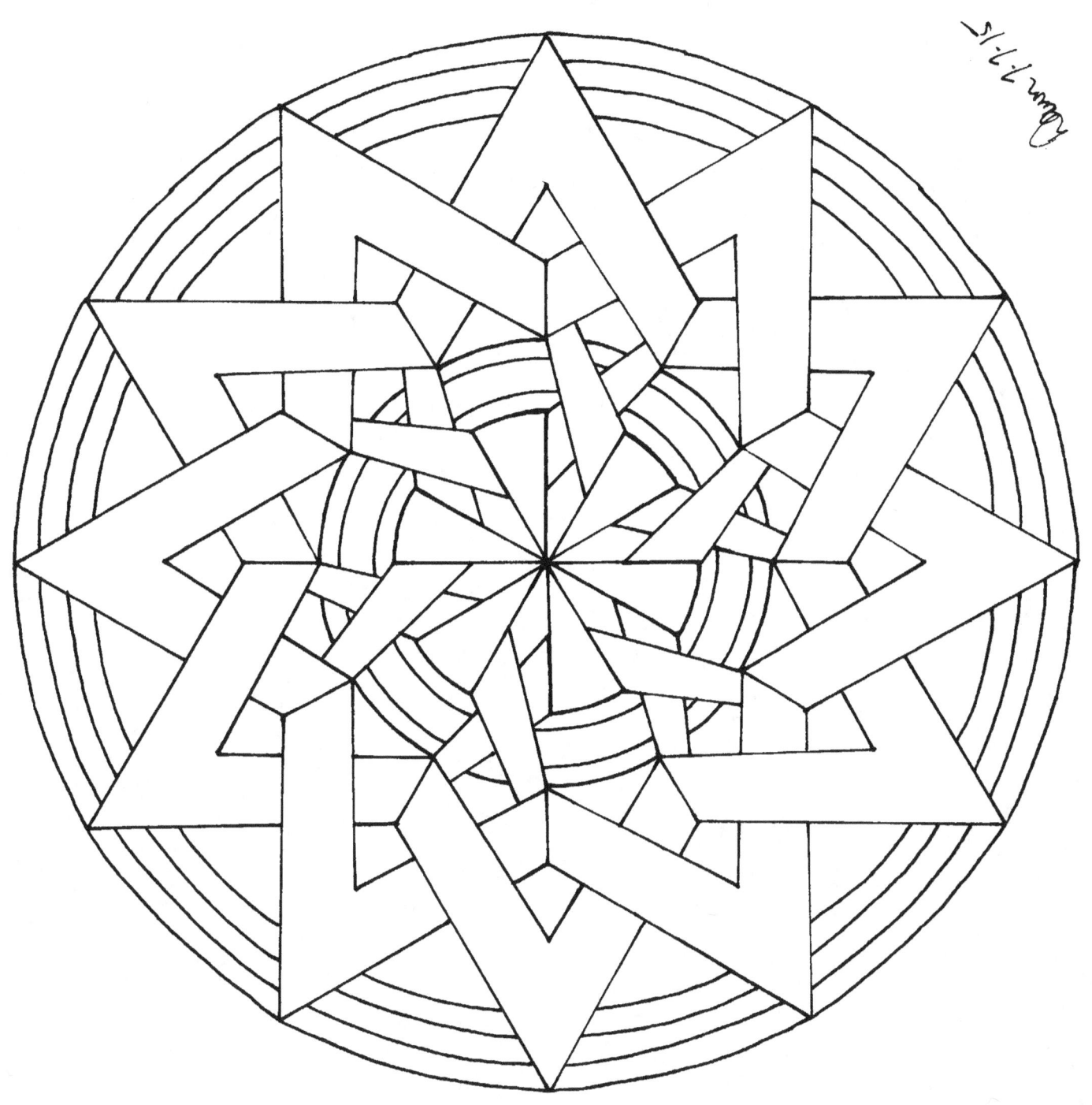

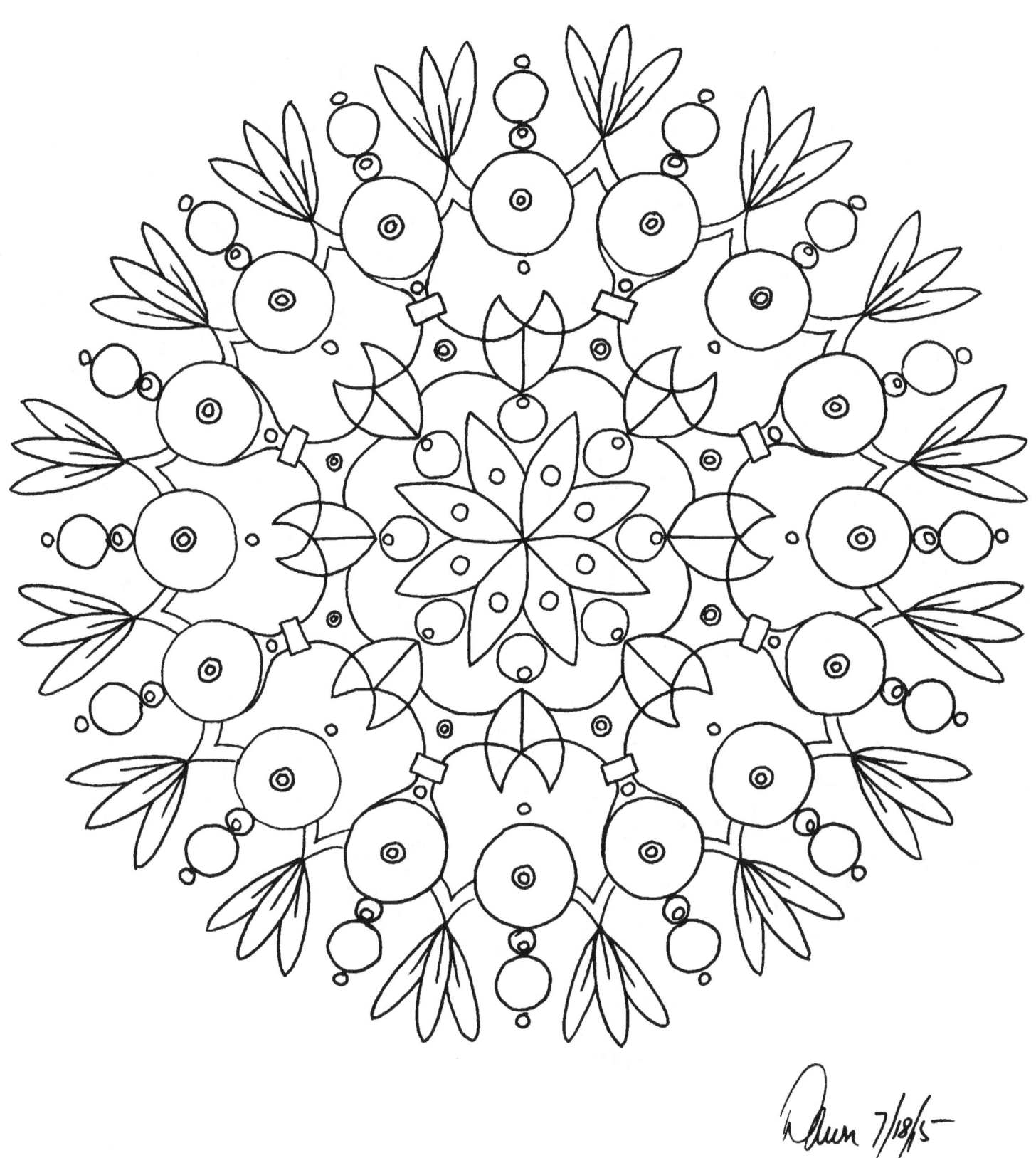

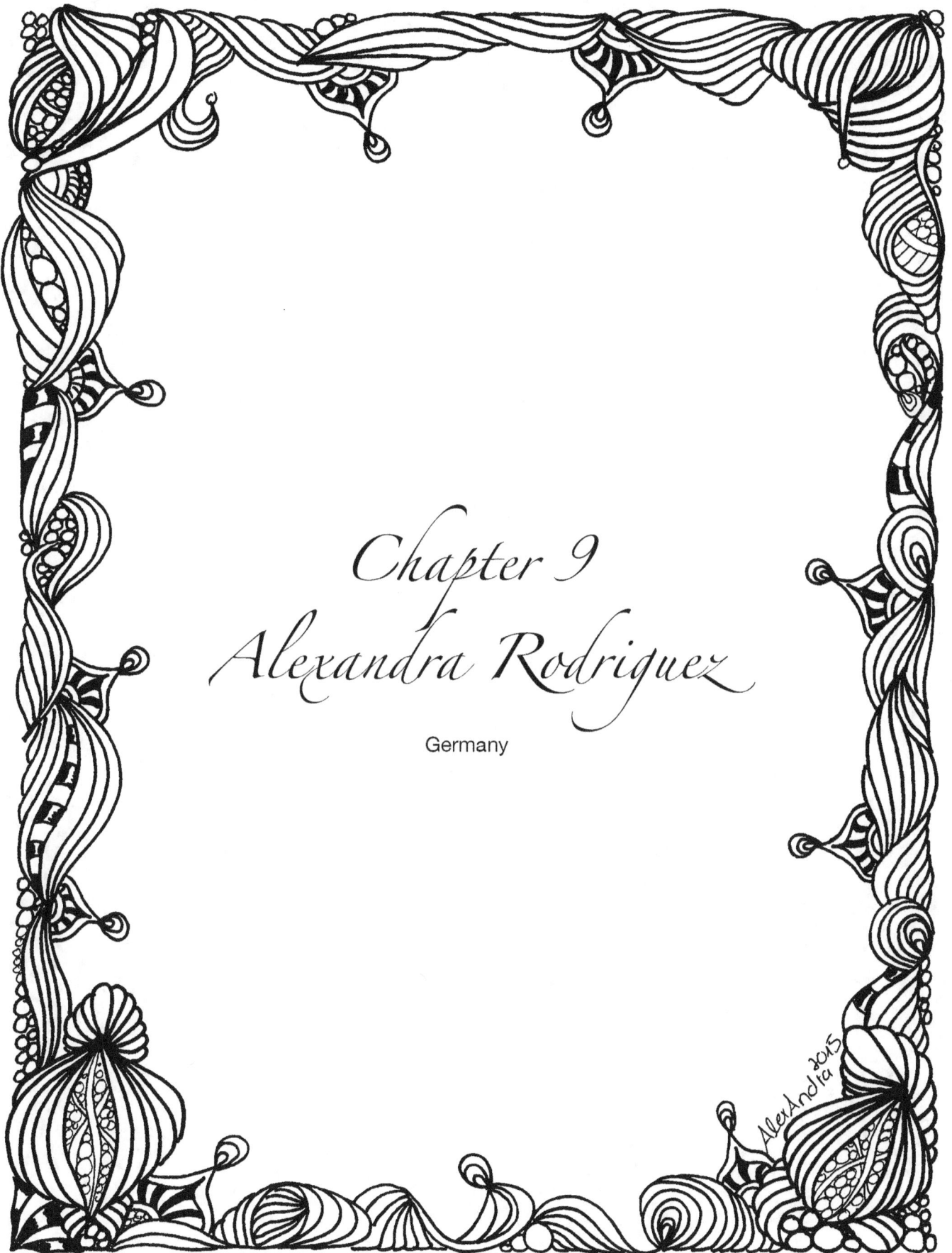

Chapter 9
Alexandra Rodriguez

Germany

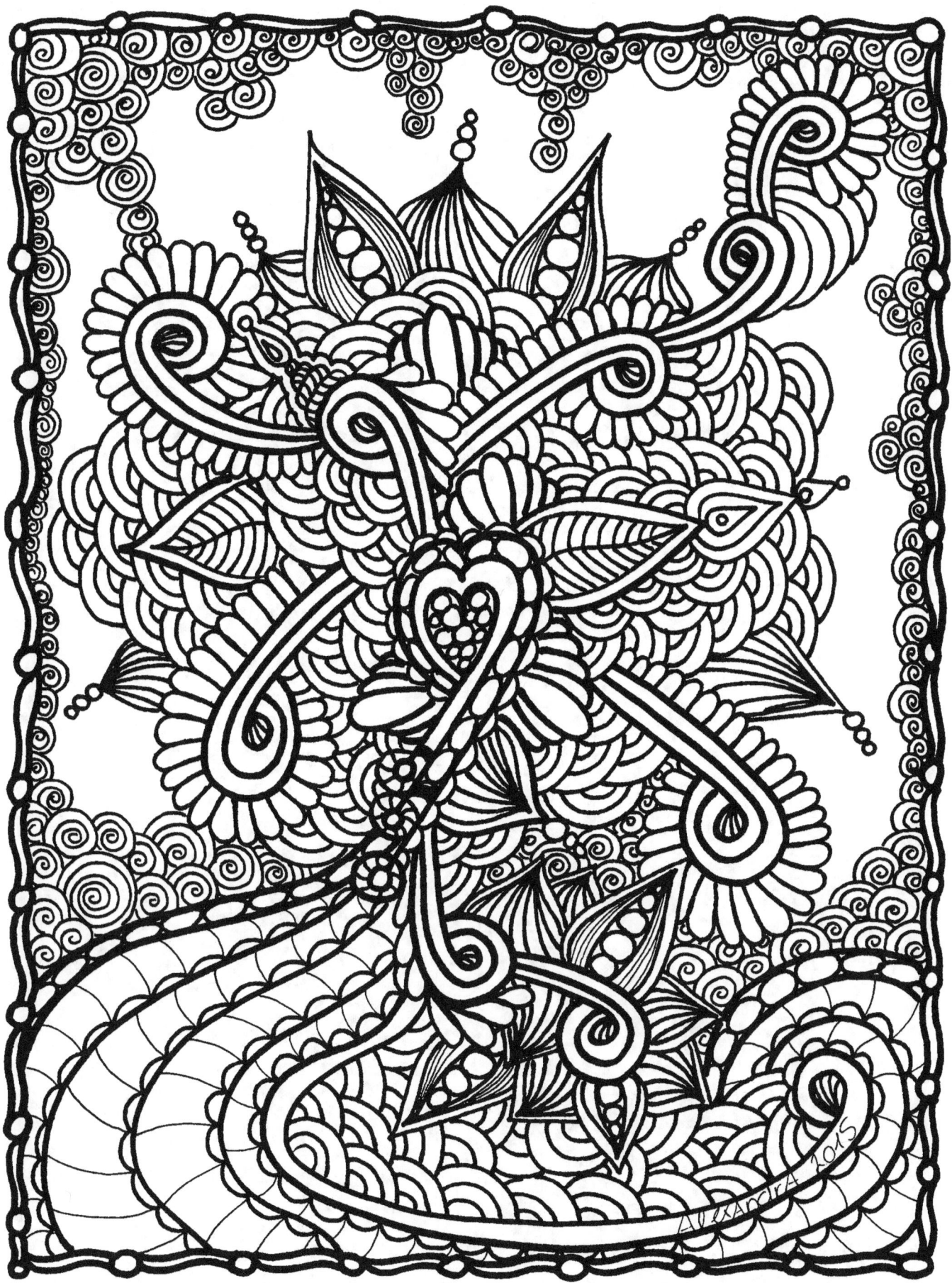

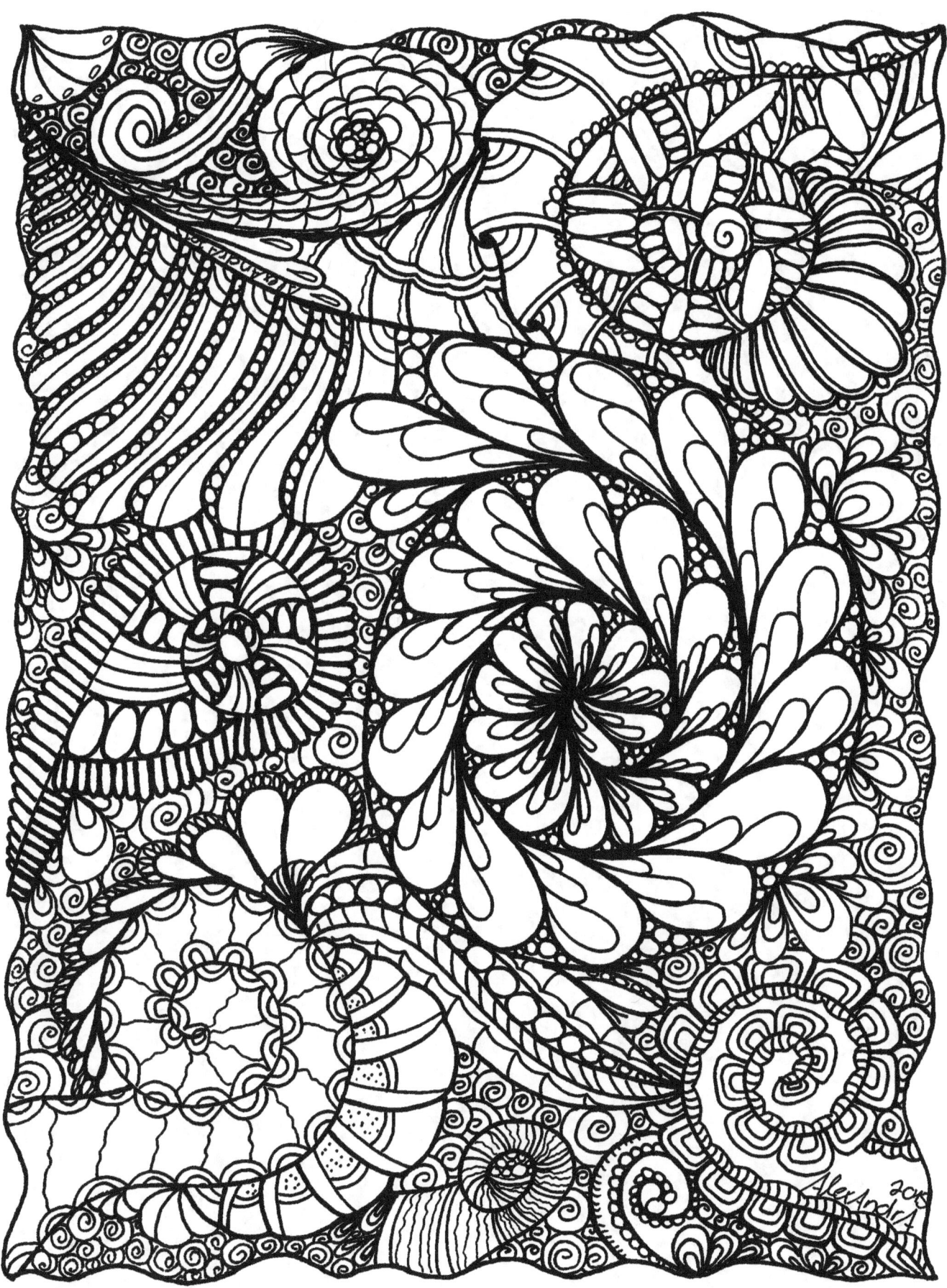

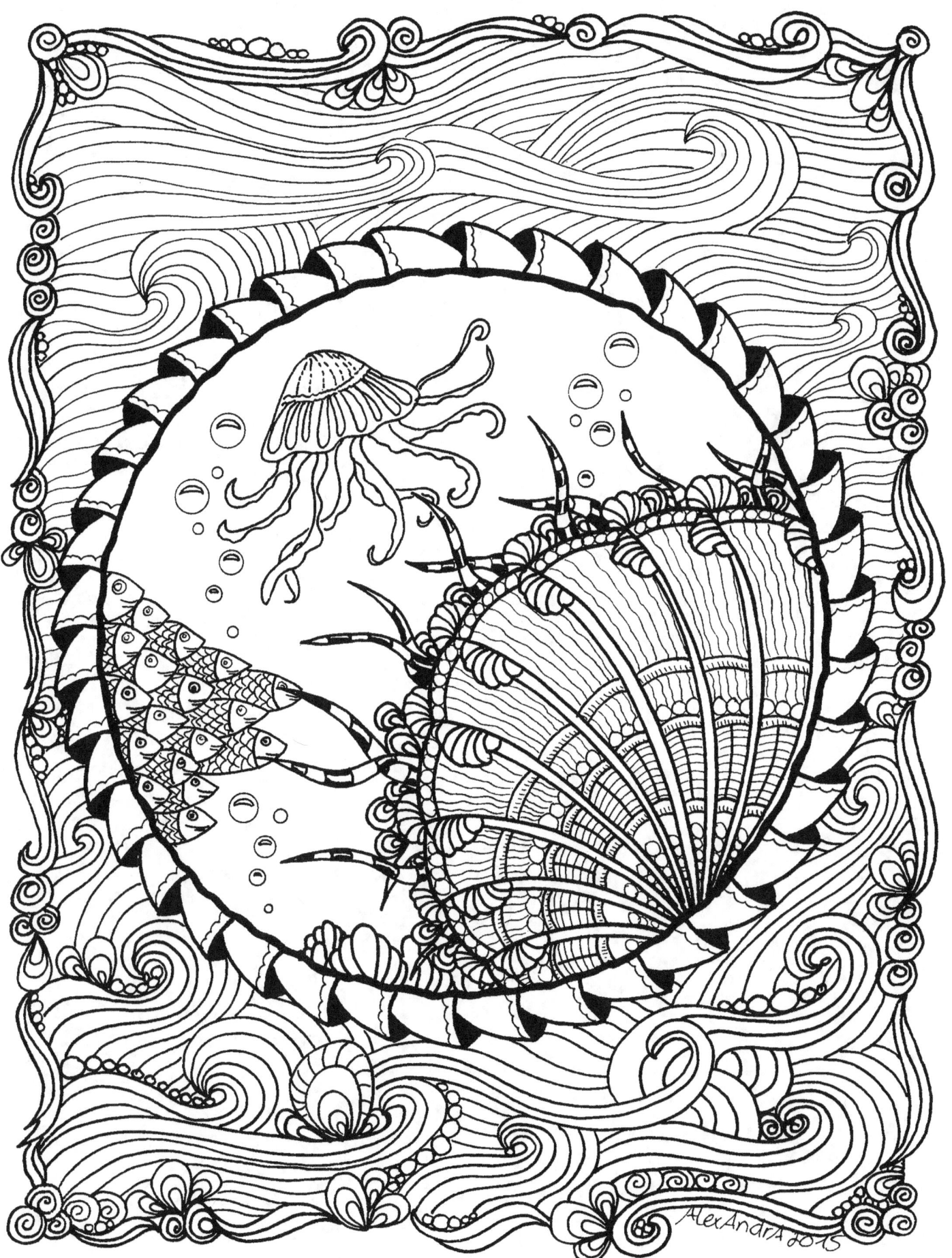

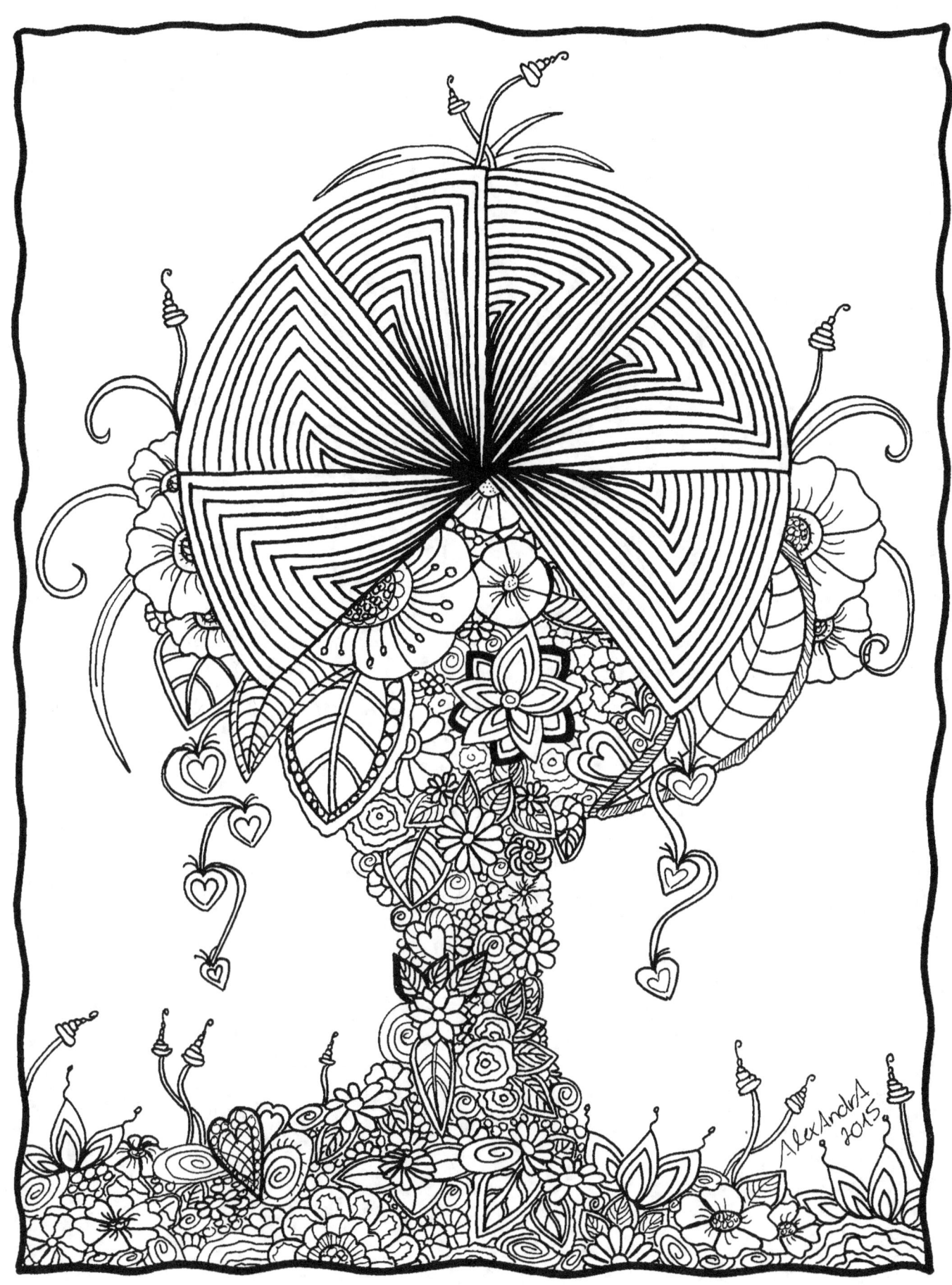

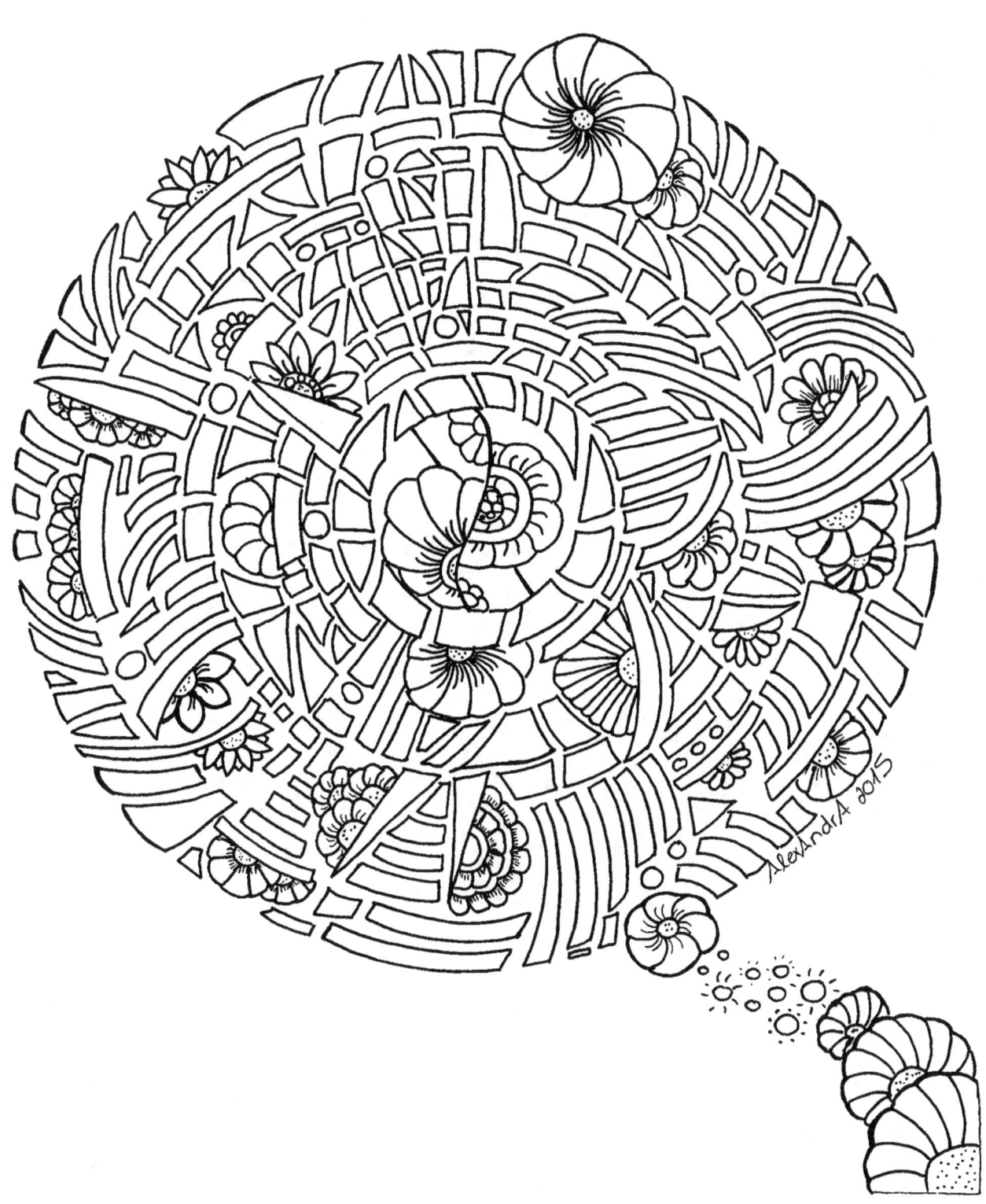

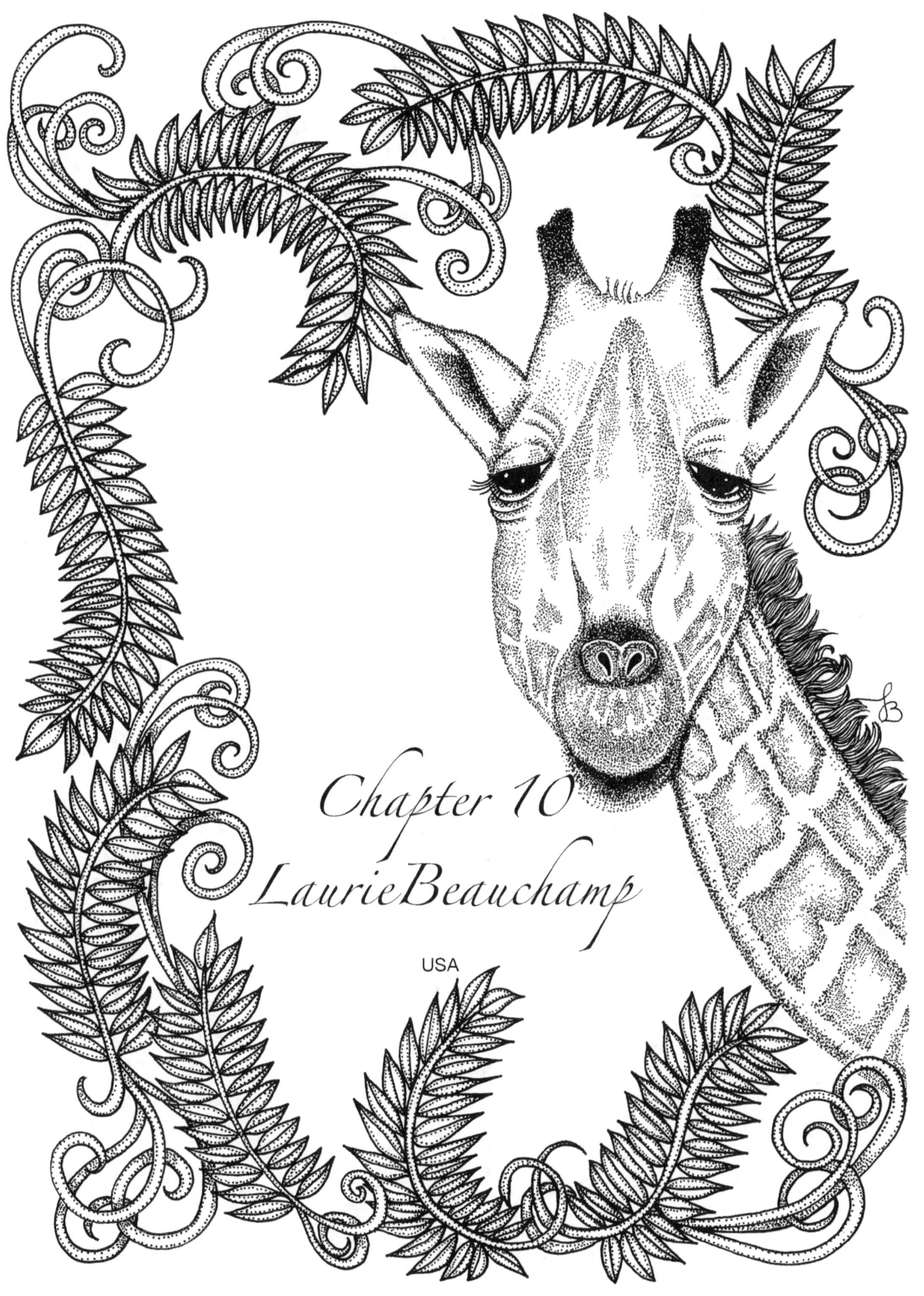

Chapter 10
Laurie Beauchamp
USA

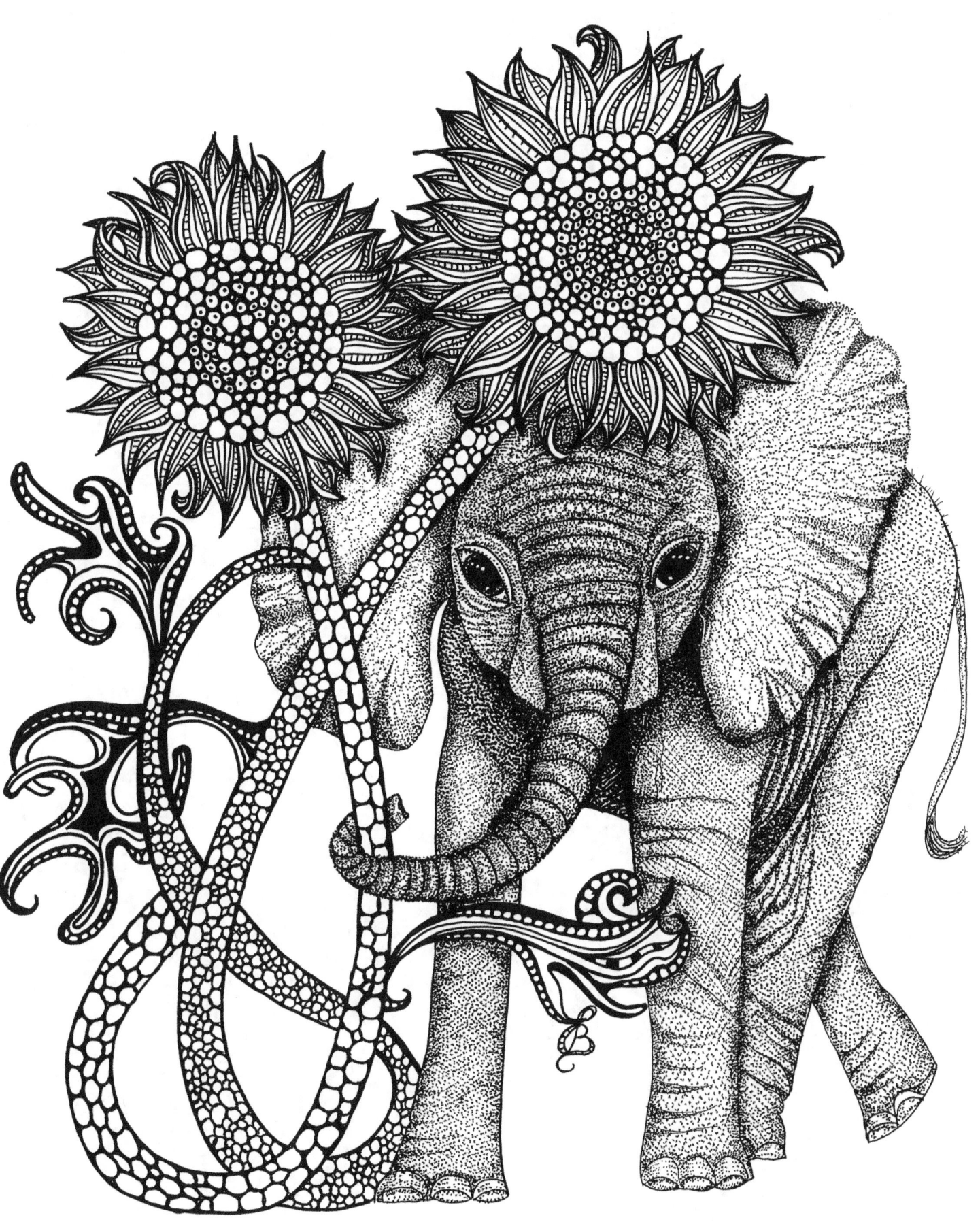

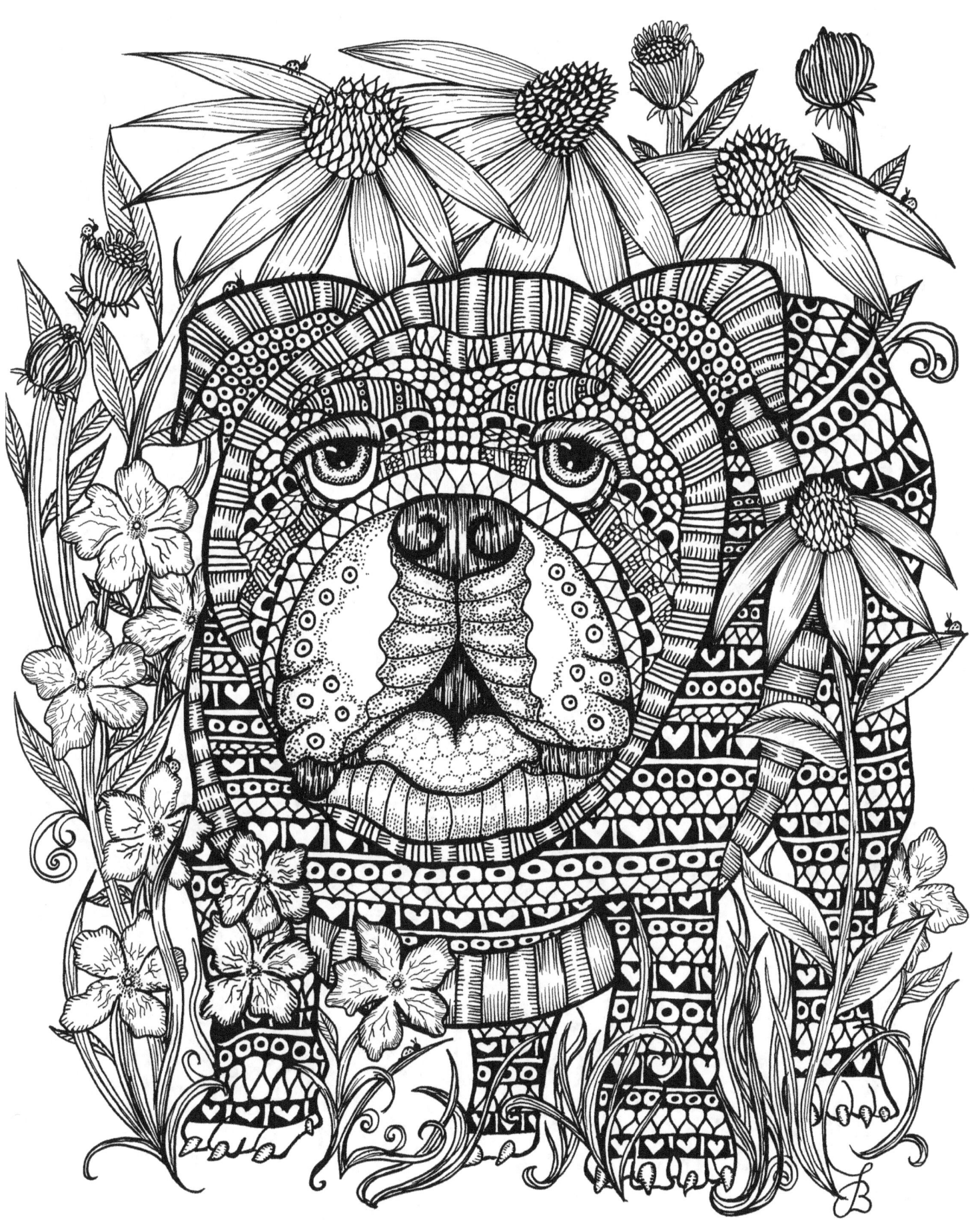

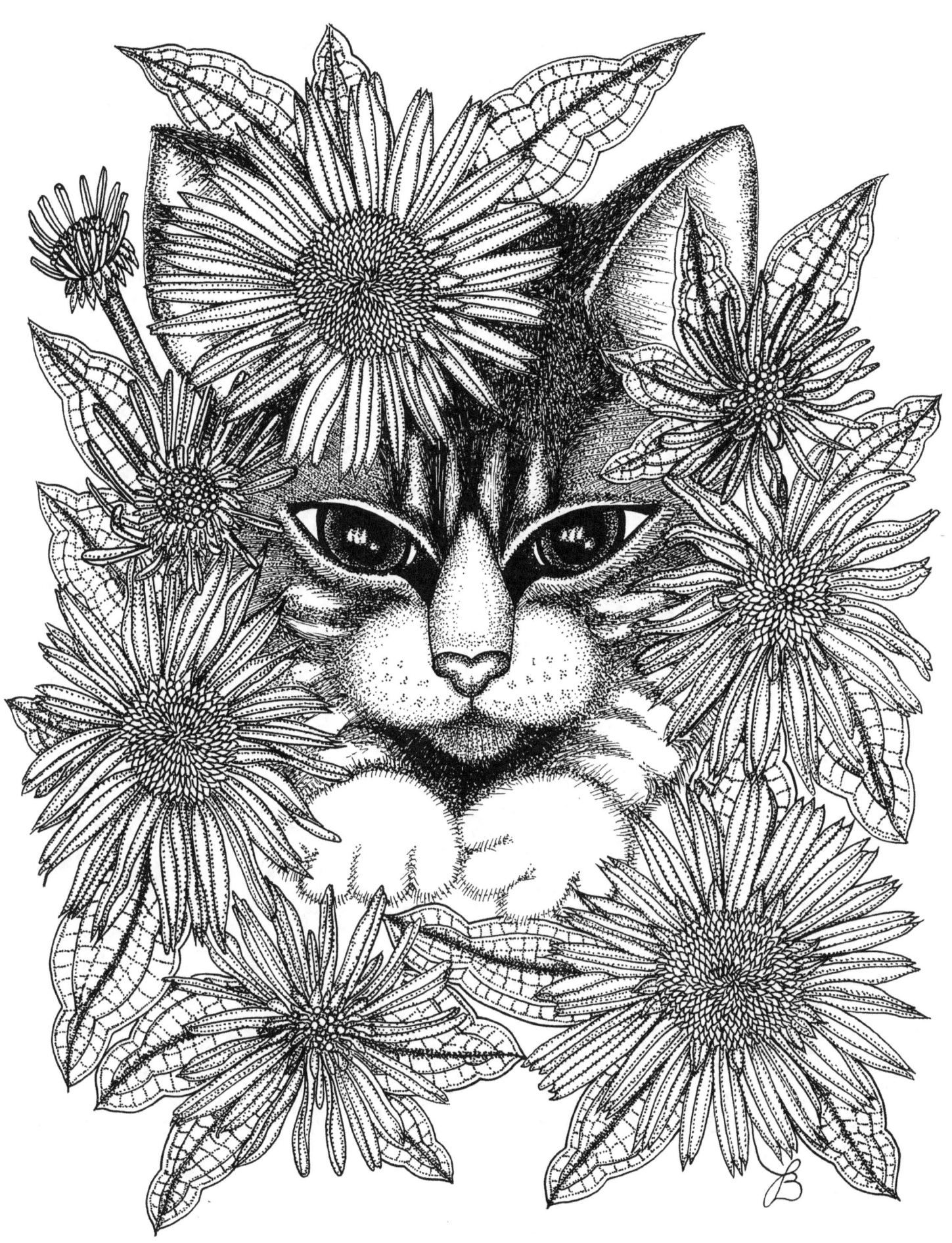

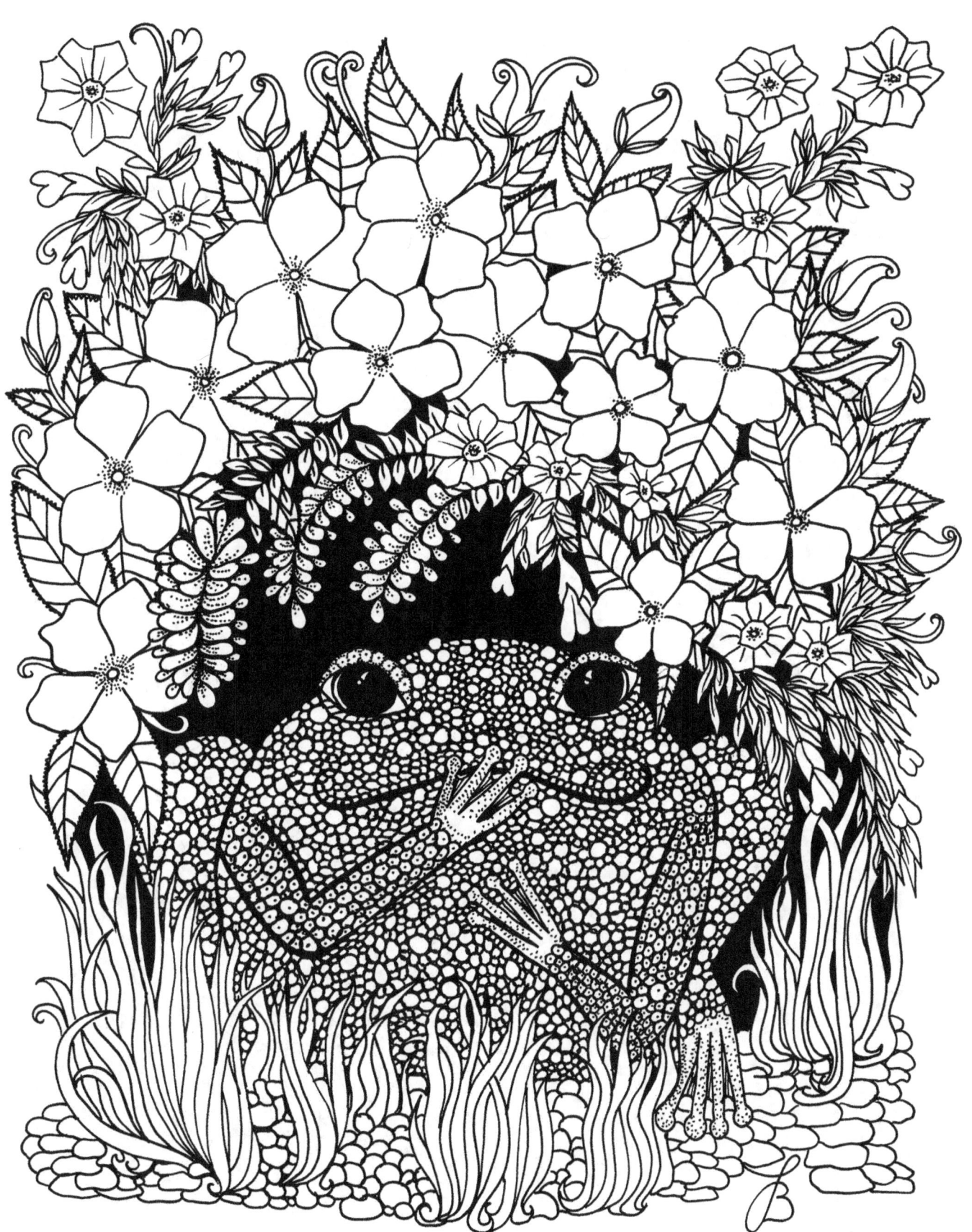

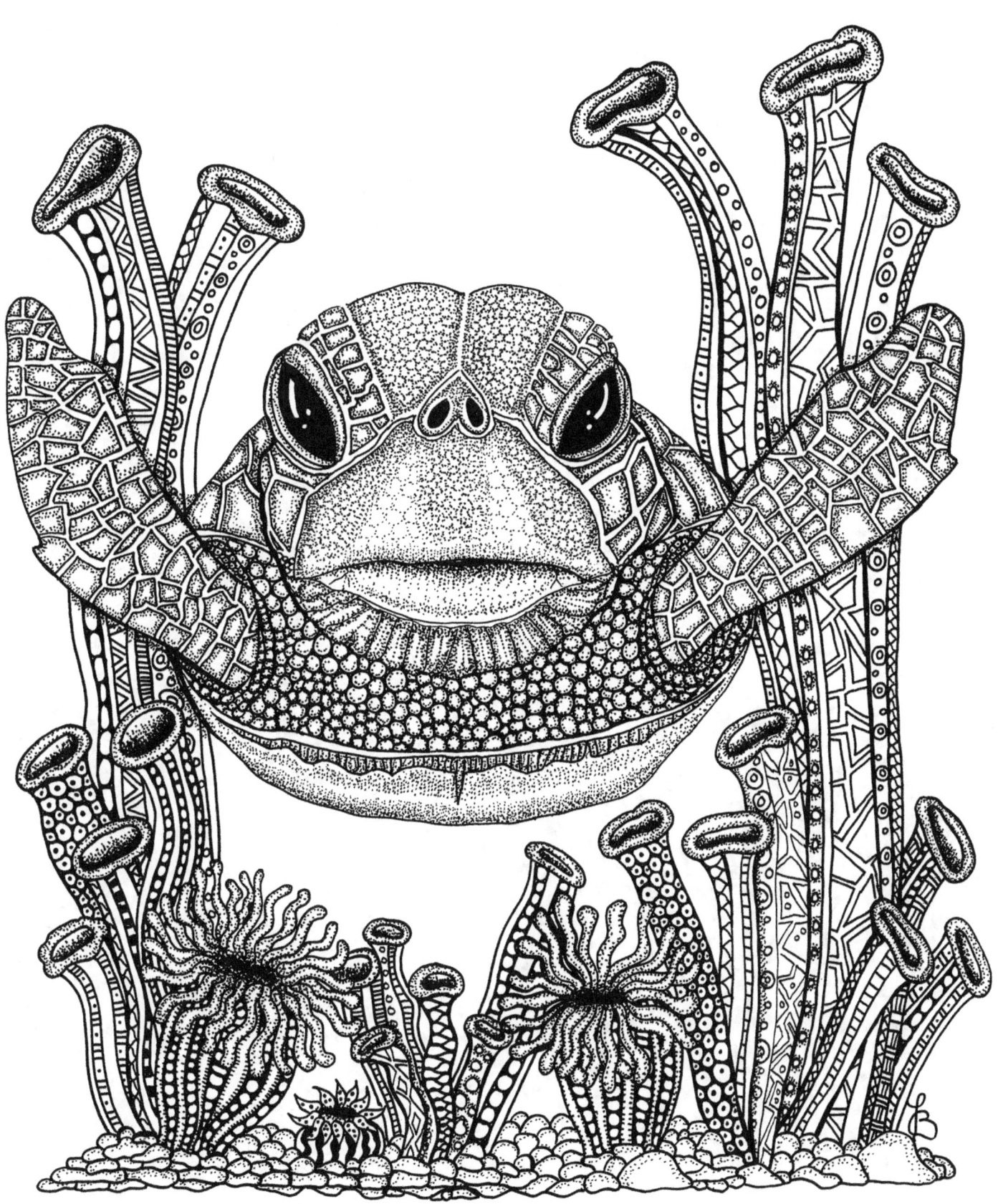

We from Global Doodle Gems, hope your journey through our book has been a pleasant one !

Please feel free to share your colored versions with us here :

https://www.facebook.com/groups/globaldoodlegems/

In our group you can meet the artists and enjoy exclusive freebies, video previews and participate in our community charity books "100 Doodles from 100 Doodlers" and so much more.... if you are wishing, that you could have the Chapter pages without the text, well then swing on by the group and get them for free in the freebie pdf for volume 6.....

Are you curious about Volume 7 ?....well, just take a look at the next 2 pages and you will know what to exspect in the next volume of "Global Doodle Gems !

"Global Doodle Gems" Volume 7
Preview

Yaya

Mitchell Manuel

Maggie Lin

Iben Lykke Højholdt

Jeanne Burbage

Marieke Raterman-Bos

Creative Rosalien

Ena Tera Art

Esther Lafiebre

Peggy Sue's Art

Meet the artists feautured in "GDG" Volume 7

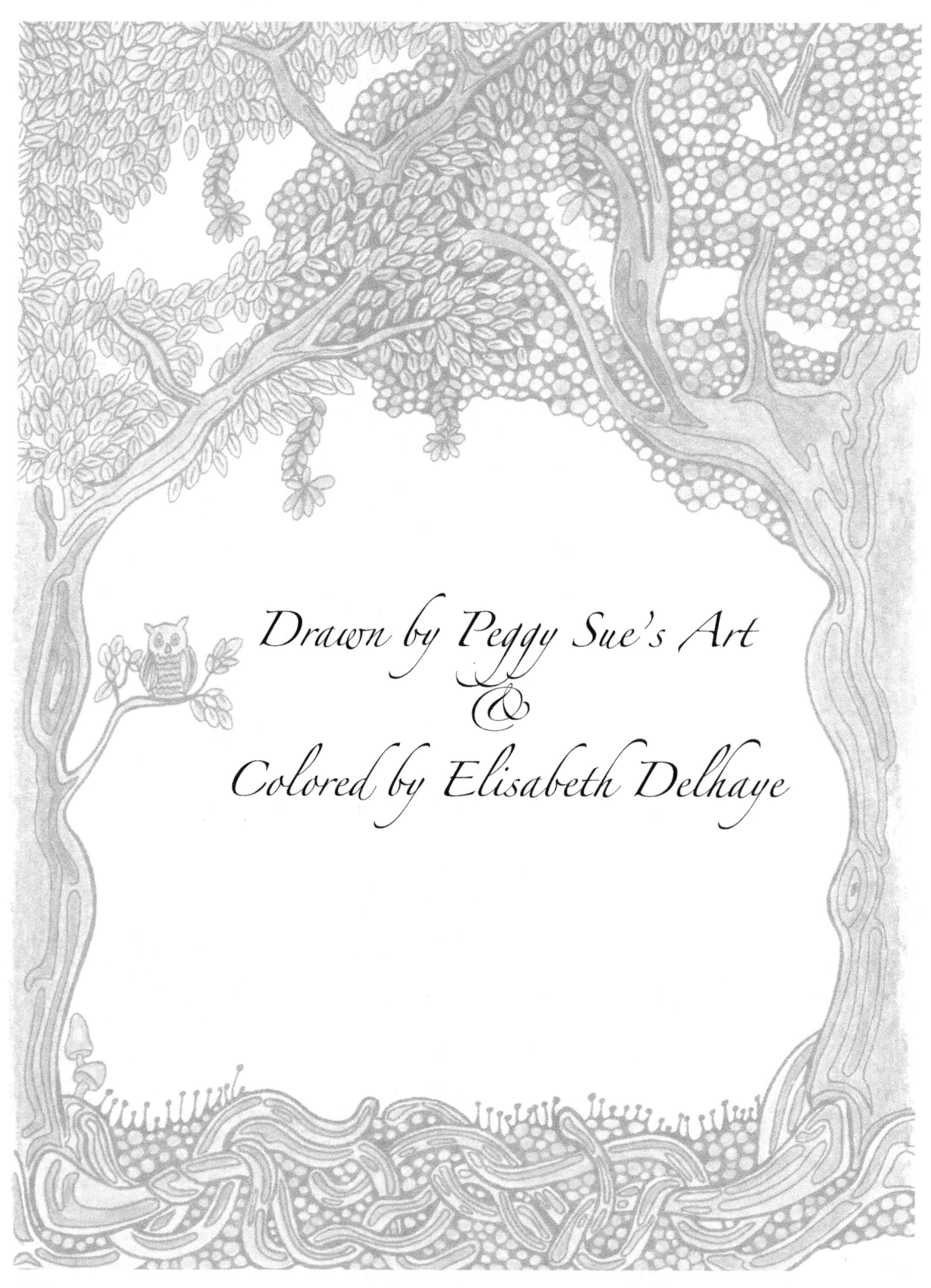

Drawn by Peggy Sue's Art
&
Colored by Elisabeth Delhaye

www.ingramcontent.com/pod-product-compliance
Lightning Source LLC
Chambersburg PA
CBHW082207220526
45470CB00010B/3077

Drawn by Orbleue's & colored by TaSo

Drawn by Jenny Wei & colored by Debbie Lai

Global Doodle Gems Volume 5
"The Ultimate international Coloring Book...an Epic Collection from Artists around the World!"

Drawn & colored by Twisted Branch Studio

Drawn & colored by Linda Karpinski

Drawn & colored by Faith Swann

Drawn & colored by Amandine Cyril ML

Drawn & colored by Mr End

Drawn & colored by Fabienne Tosi

Drawn & colored by T.J.

Drawn & colored by Lynni Ex

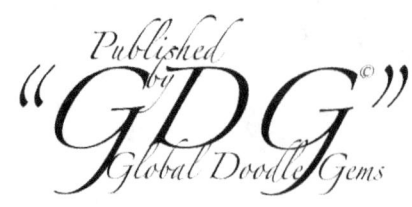

Share your colored versions with us ! We love seeing your results and hearing from you we are social !

The Official FB book page, stay on top of what we have in the works !
www.facebook.com/globaldoodlegems

The Community group, share your colored pages, meet the artists, enjoy exclusive freebies, take part in community Charity books and so much more......
www.facebook.com/groups/globaldoodlegems/

Follow us on Twitter.... @GlobalDoodlegem

We are on Instagram too
@globaldoodlegems for instagram

...and if you are not social like that we have a blog
globaldoodlegems.wordpress.com

Copyright © 2015 Global Doodle Gems

All rights are reserved by Global Doodle Gems.

Duplication of pages for personal use are allowed. You are invited to color the pages then scan/post your coloured versions to social networks, mentioning the book title and author/artist (Global Doodle Gems).

All artwork and images are protected by copyright laws. This book or any portion thereof may not, otherwise, be reproduced and/or distributed or transmitted without the express written permission of the artist/publisher of Global Doodle Gems.

All of us from the Global Doodle Gems wish you a colortastic time and look forward to seeing your wonderful color results online !